Praise for
McTlàn

Alvarez goes on a sick one to gift us a tall can wrapped in a brown bag collection. *McTlán* relentlessly journeys into the underworld to reclaim the ancient and dismantle the present. From the visual glyphs to the sprawling "slanguage" tongues of La Muerte, La Llorona, Tlāloc, and those submerged in the "Amurkan" empire, Alvarez embodies the grand-channeler able to see anew, lest you, the reader, "find yrself muy dead." Here, is the "(m)Al Norte" ideal exposed, unique to the vision and hallucination that only Alvarez can summon.

— **Anthony Cody**, author of *Borderland Apocrypha*
winner of a 2021 American Book Award

Steven Alvarez's new collection is a kinetic and yummy and vital contribution to the canon of Latinx vispo. *McTlan*'s bluehot and polyglot vision quest propelled me forward into the next dimension a la Herrera, a la Gomez-Pena. This book is a love song to the cabronx heart that pulses despite the squeeze of the capitalist fists of the Yoonaited Estaytes de Amurka. Ooof, this book blows my mind.

— **Carmen Giménez Smith**, poet and author of *Cruel Futures*
and *Bring Down the Little Birds*, winner of a 2011 American Book Award

Mctlàn

FLOWERSONG
PRESS

by
Steven Alvarez

FLOWERSONG
PRESS

FlowerSong Press
Copyright © 2022 by Steven Alvarez
ISBN: 978-1-953447-60-9
Library of Congress Control Number: 2022930378

Published by FlowerSong Press
in the United States of America.
www.flowersongpress.com

Cover Art by Walter Jaczkowski
Cover Art Design by Walter Jaczkowski

NOTICE: SCHOOLS AND BUSINESSES
FlowerSong Press offers copies of this book at quantity discount with bulk
purchase for educational, business, or sales promotional use. For information, please email the
Publisher at info@flowersongpress.com.

CONTENTS

ENTER OZTOTL...IN THE BEGINNING THE McDEAD

WALLED / MURALS 20

TELENOVELA MATERIAL Y LA VIDA CABRONA 76

LA LLORONA IN MAMHATITLAN 82

IF 84

XOCHITL SONG 86

Y LA PELONA 88

LAND OF RED DAYLIGHT 2 96

& WHEN ATE MANAGED HANDS CLUMSILY 103

Q YE ASKED A 123

A HUEVO McOYE

C SURROUNDED 132

OYE 139

McCUICATL 144

LA LLORONA BE RIGHT 154

McCOWARDS

UNO 163

DOS 175

DOS PUNTO CINCO 177

TRES 178

McCUATRO 182

YR POCHX IS THIS

    & VISION VISION   199

    IN XOCHITL IN CUICATL   215

    CANTO FLORIDA UKASA XOCHICUICATL   255

    SUN RISES SUN SETS   277

    2008 / 5TH SUN / OUR PRESENT   279

TONALAMATLLY

    NOSOSTROS LOS AMURIKANOS   286

    CRY BABY CRY   289

    SD CHALEY   293

    LA PELONA   304

    EVERYBODY KNOWS THERE'S ONE NOGALES   307

    REMNANT OF PERSONAL COMMUNICATION

        ULISES CHASTITELLEZ   309

    & LEAVE EM / AINT WORTH YR TIME / WALK EM   311

    FUTILE SEARCH FOR ORIGINS   323

    AMURKUS   324

    LULAC . W. SHELLAc & SAND   334

    MESS-TE HACES?   344

ACKNOWLEDGEMENTS   357

La tierra no hace reproches

Dijo su madre en un rezo

Porque del polvo saliste

Tendrás que cubrir tu cuerpo

Que Dios perdone tus actos

Después rezó un Padre Nuestro

LOS TIGRES DEL NORTE

for every verse that curls up in my people's chest

i win five libraries from the enemy.

RAQUEL SALAS RIVERA

Zás

ALURISTA

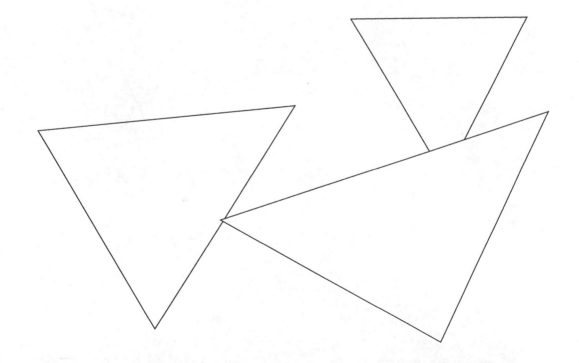

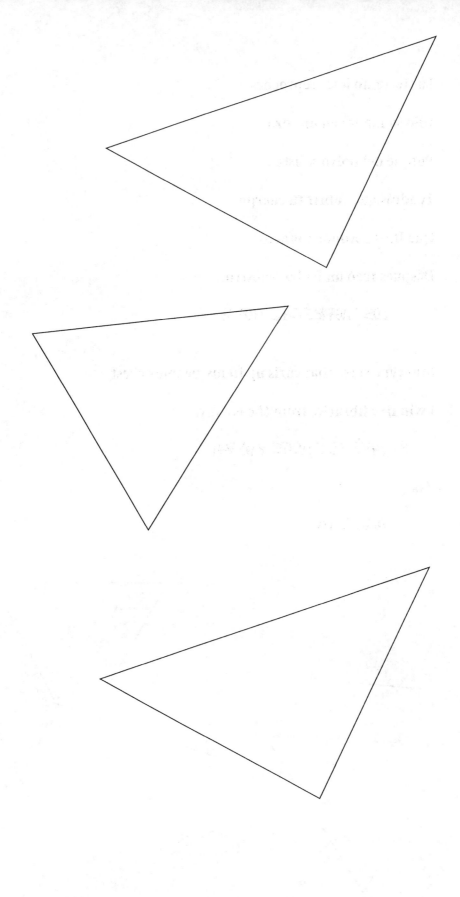

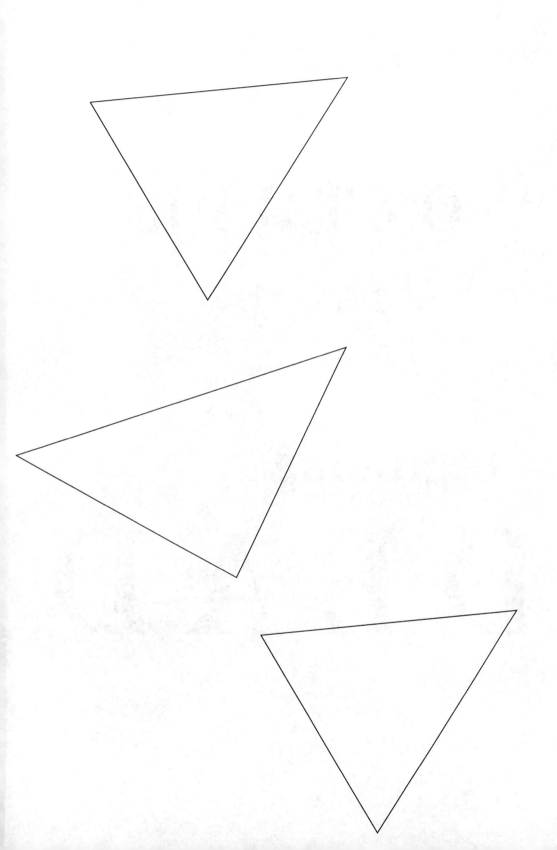

ENTER

OZTOTL

◆ ◆ ◆

in the

beginning the

DEAD

(5) D

(6) De

(7) De es

(8) De indio

(9) De lobo e

(11) De cambujo

(13) De barquino y

(16) De coyote, mestiz

verdad y only to bend reckonings   & sand & brown heat

. bowing vacant horizon   gritted pendulum

McTlán is the dry lot   lo this is the dry lot

but

there
tan bonita for

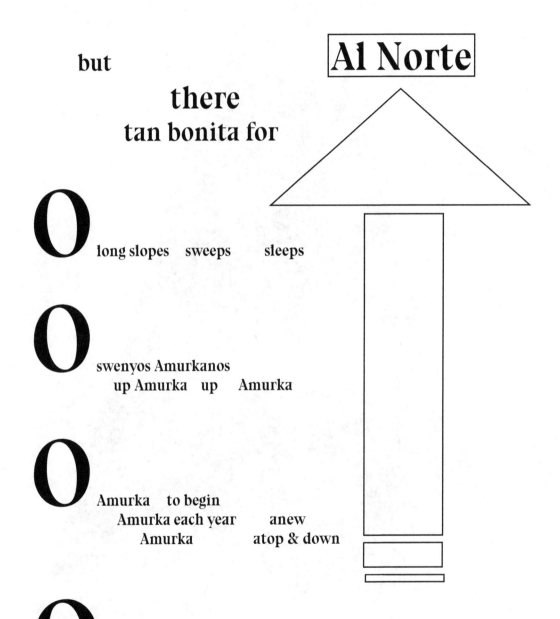

Al Norte

O long slopes   sweeps   sleeps

O swenyos Amurkanos
up Amurka   up   Amurka

O Amurka   to begin
Amurka each year   anew
Amurka   atop & down

O unceasing Amurka   in Amurka all's leyenda
salieron los Chastitellez   pasaron los Panchos
Al Norte yr dreamvisions Amurkanenses

c   a   m   p   a   n   a

M<CHINGACHINGACHINGG<CHING

[here media res that ol McChinga maching Meshika]

x & x . . . rested . . . on both sides . . . cosmic

árbol . . . rooted at center . . . surrounded by

underworld divine waters . . . & stellar

branches of milky starclouds /

estrellasyelos . . . veins to nebulae . . . veins

& nebulae & these heft heaven . . . bracketed

by 2 plumed coatls drooling fertility . . .

       & our xá . . . & our xá . . .

carved into solar stelae . . . & still eternal

night . . . & sky sweated rain onto forests

blooming . . . see this universe established

/ destroyed / reestablished . . . times . . . 4 . .

. maybe 5 . . . depending who ye ask . . .

testimonies of Suns . . . & our xá Tonantzin

& our xá Totahtzin together entwined ...

¡OMETEOTL!

& out plops Messico & AZtlán

¡YO ME! ¡YO MY!
yepa epyiofiayoo &

these serpents slither together

perpendicular & suddenly our

Dios en Dios Ometeotl—begetter /

conceiver—bends into ... xá Guadalupe ...

& our xá compa Chuy

garbed in slimed red & pyrite & greenblue

w. yellow trim

bien chingón sequins y todo

/ & w.. nothing sd not meant

& behold from below . apron

& Chaley Chastitellez's roots

roving further northward ...

comiença del segundo dark libro: que trata
de los antepasados y sacrificios y solenjdades:
que estos naturals desta McTlán hazian: a
honrra de sus chorizos

ponese al cabo deste libro por via de apendiz:
los edificios y oficios y chingaderas y
serujcios y oficiales que auja en el templo
mexicanx

WALLED

MURALS

aint death bc ever'one

knows La Muerte

got   c i o & c i e ed ch h s ¿mande?

¿como ves? ¿yes? yes

Mc chi u l y con c r cr d

¿como ves? ¿yes?

weird as fuck   bless

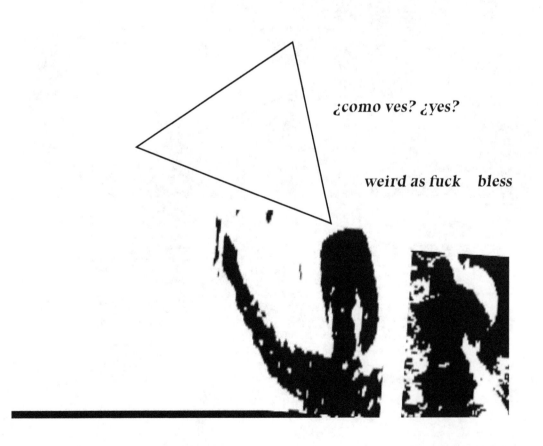

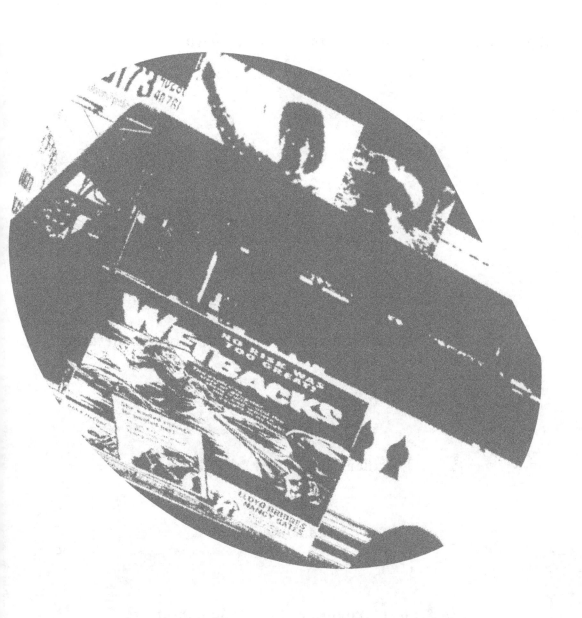

oye watcha I can make it verse ea r ese

look q i a u p nch c r de a a

& get on next   camionsototototote   a huevo

make it
rain
Tlaloc

back to yr p nch cas cha de mostly of maderuca

yepa   ahem that is

& suddenly piqué

con El no Pal puntiagudo   no indeed

but sweat Y futuro

La Pelona & Chaley ChastItllez acarameladOs

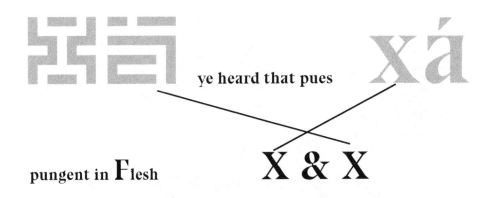

ye heard that pues

xá

pungent in Flesh

X & X

& as turns head toward la puerta

there stands achInchincle holding An accordion

& an uzi   sunglasses & sombrero & tan cotton-polY suit

sO O1 Chaley rests head agachóned

right after all ye're   the arquitonto of all this

mechanics of cabrón   eipyiofiayoo eipyiofiayoo

poet vomit

¿ 'member song ?

that ol' cuicatl

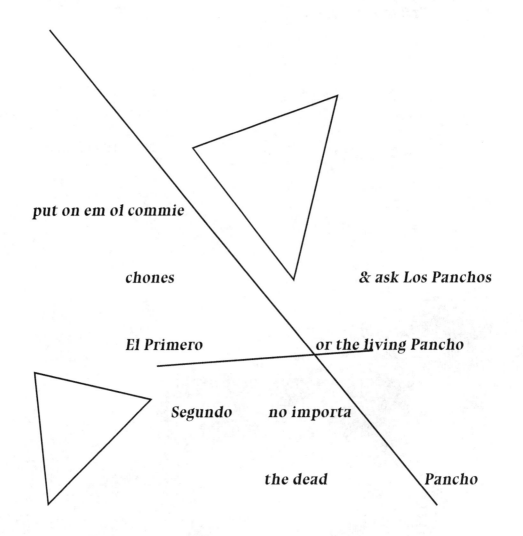

put on em ol commie

chones   & ask Los Panchos

El Primero   or the living Pancho

Segundo   no importa

the dead   Pancho

paddle further into brambles

nahuas play w. agave pencas

nappin as one livin

        & canopies of

        nopales &

        hammocks unfurl

NOPAL NOPAL NOPAL NOPAL NOPAL NOPAL NOPAL NOPAL NOPAL

w.

bodies

freeholayro

dream

Myyy—self done

waitin for work

workin   makin worth

old   schools homes factories

that ol'   Amurka rusted

from   inside out

wheredoespoetrycomefrom—

visions   bueno visions

& from   recognition & facility

& post   industrial intellectual labor

learning to labor over wordswords

see any work written work

zero poetry policy sey myyy—self sacrificed

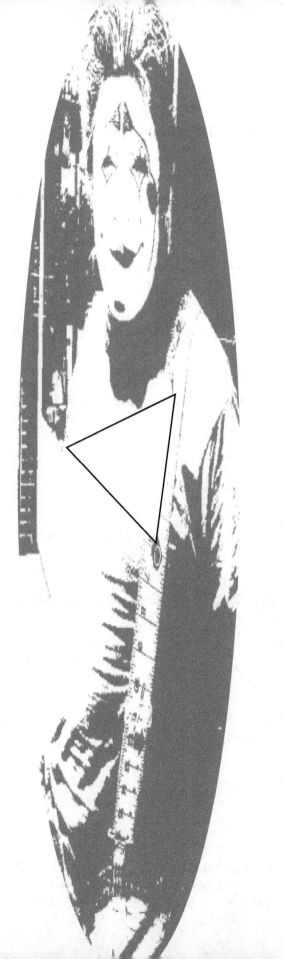

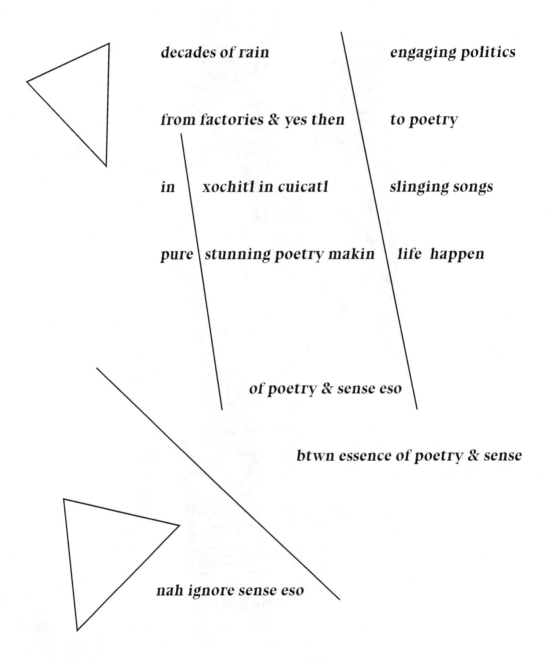

here history   hear this extraordinary morning

tired dirty happy pouring brown rain*

decades of rain   engaging politics

from factories & yes then   to poetry

in   xochitl in cuicatl   slinging songs

pure stunning poetry makin life happen

of poetry & sense eso

btwn essence of poetry & sense

nah ignore sense eso

---

* rain from ground up Alaxsxsa. Amerindian poet sd to someone in AZtlán who
sd this to Chaley as Chaley imagined such rain dripping coldly brownly from
everything / staining everything cold & wind to lift . & green green ¡GO!

so mister President Nenoqujch on bigger than life TV
there for me | hoła sir | hello | name's Pansho Chastitellez
| you might remember me from such poems as "2008 /
5th sun / our present" wherein my sobrino Chaey
Chastitllez dumped my ashes in a flowerpot in Times
Esquare of Manhatitlán | never heard of it | no hay pena |
bueno ye got to fund it | see I'm trying to do a bad
gringo accent & . swagger Ooh man | just want to be
pyrite like you capitán | number one team in Amurka
they're playing making great | again | fuck that | they're
playing good | got nietos mister President Nenoqujch |
sure are big too | oh yeah | they get the visions too | yeah
| Quetzalcoatl bless you mister President Nenoqujch
| mister President Nenoqujch ¿do you know my sister
Malinshay Marina? | hey hey | hey | snazzy place | . like
it | blue tie | mister President Nenoqujch | ¿come estas?
| here dig this out for me & look | mouth | appreciate yr
support | hey | hug | had dinner w. | last night | yr're
hangin w. good company | signing more books |
autographs | mister President Nenoqujch . want gold ye
know | generally accept my praises | stand on by | stand
by | sd stand on by different views of this evening's
proceedings

here's part   *here's a part*

it is   it's eso es

espere   espere   espere   spirit

qué diablos está pasando   in this carajo

illustrated

poemstorybook   ~~glad ye asked~~

& inspire   sponsorship of

Los Chastitellez

& **Los Panchos** to scribble secret   codices

sometimes true but mostly prophesies

confirming certain inequities & social

theories & song & moja'odicus dispatches

from AZtlán everywhere & gray too & smelled

purple fabuloso freshness & brutality & harshness

& love   breathed all deep & all rushed

blissfully rain continually rain brown rain deep

into rain ran down sides of ojos

mud down dripping south from the place of misty sky

to **AridZone**   bluehot dryness

into hot redrocks jutting from brown sand

& these mountains moradas mold

delicately interrupting vast ocean of tierra

held   secluded from desert sky for in AZtlán AZtlán

sky mayn't be hid from

buildin   ol calli of Messican mem'ries

& those deep outward social relationships poesy constructed

facing both inward toward convention to stylen

Chále

voy a

borrarme

al mono con

la xalaca

~~McTlán | al Norte | AZtlán~~

vivid sickened desert   sand   heat   vacancy come in

                  Quetzalcoatl   copy that

no eres betwixt or btwn cabrón

        brace yrself coz   the Mex next to más

           & images flicker & pass pos

        mucho maas deeper mero pues   eipyiofiayoo

¿ye want carnitas ?   ye'd better respect aGuad-loop ¿eh?

¿no respeto?   & send ye right to yr—

okay then drop a fucking

vision

some underworld mystic dead chigadera

_____

* yup   get ready for more of that

magical realism booshit but mebbe poesy

& pos example of this

well F that & anyway yr President Nenoqujch passed

& these verses return to wanderings

no doubt ye noticed

see & patrilineal heritage of Chastitellez

held tradition

of going hellward every generation poetry

music flowers treasure much to be of stolen riches

& destruction

& a heap of slanguage

& epik chubasco of McTlán

& there upon

fewer postcards

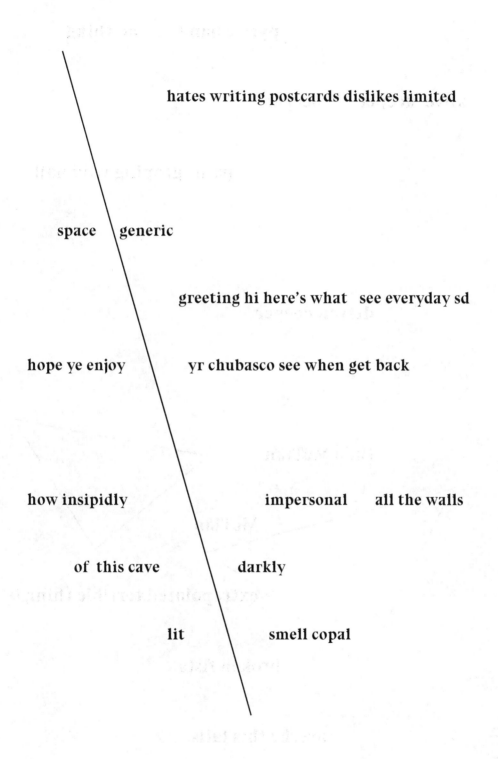

hates writing postcards dislikes limited

space   generic

greeting hi here's what   see everyday sd

hope ye enjoy   yr chubasco see when get back

how insipidly   impersonal   all the walls

of this cave   darkly

lit   smell copal

pyrite hand   no thing

alive deeper   deeper

                 pain groping wild nail

driven deeper

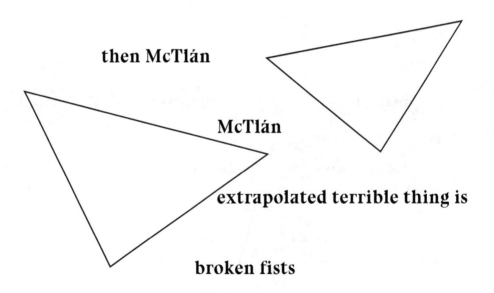

then McTlán

          McTlán

           extrapolated terrible thing is

       broken fists

maybe this falls

from broken fists

& sweaty brows forget broken fists Chaley

gripping pit deeper still yet

further deep into McTlán

& humbleness two tumbleweeds

broken fists

branched in   union

branched

McTlán   McTlán   broken   fists

broken as one   one sickness

dry   deeper

fist

broken

fist &

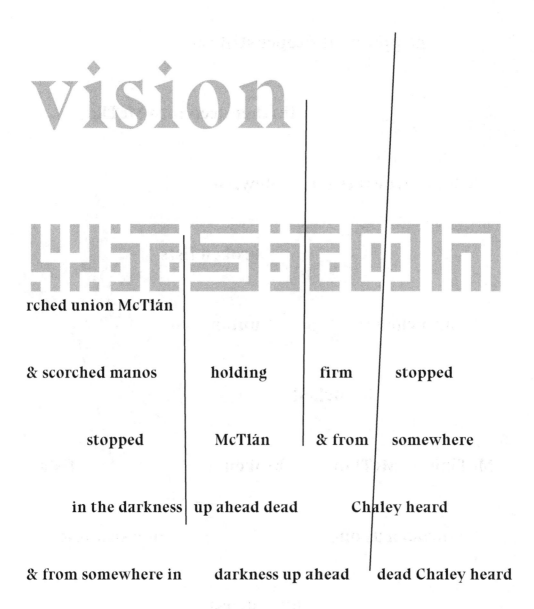

vision

rched union McTlán

& scorched manos   holding   firm   stopped

stopped   McTlán   & from   somewhere

in the darkness up ahead dead   Chaley heard

& from somewhere in   darkness up ahead   dead Chaley heard

¿how calm wd one feel?

¿how scorned?

¿how   separated?

then down loosed   deep & deeper into
plumpy shit McTlán

¿how learned?

O   McTlán   O McTlán   Chaley   muy
      muerto   güey

alas all wd   sez   sez

sey cess   sez sez

alas

O   McTlán

alas general dismay   alas

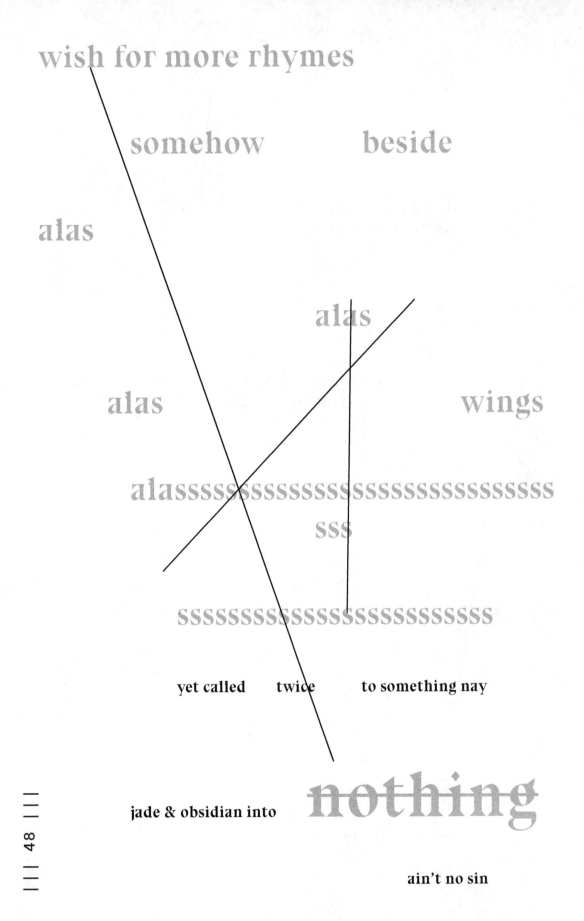

wish for more rhymes

somehow   beside

alas

alas

alas   wings

alassssssssssssssssssssssssssssssssss
sss

sssssssssssssssssssssssssssssss

yet called   twice   to something nay

nothing

jade & obsidian into

ain't no sin

take away yr skin

                                          & walk walk

        walk away in yr huesos

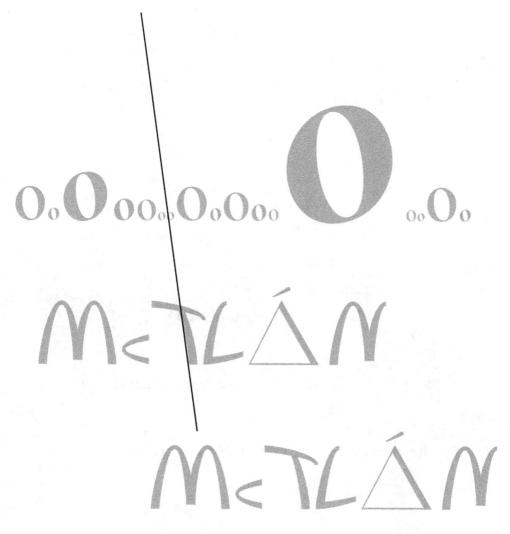

before arriving   in

nothing

Mc TLÁN

(m)aL nORTE

AZtlán

dismay

dismay general   to

no dismay   Chaley arrived presently—

vision

deeper into

pool of cess McTlán   skyscrapers & shadows
smoking   obsidian

mirrors upward looked noticing   infinity

docked   nearby others stopped   all saw how
water held infinity resting on whaleroad

all   saw how

||| 51 |||

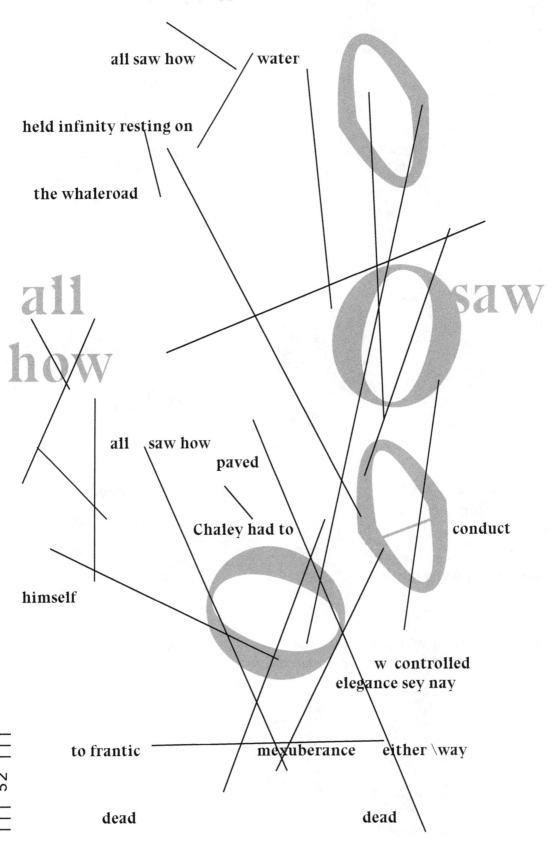

others stopped to marvel as well

all saw how   water

held infinity resting on

the whaleroad

all

how

saw

all   saw how

paved

Chaley had to   conduct

himself

w controlled
elegance sey nay

to frantic   mexuberance   either \way

dead   dead

made way up toward

of earth little

swell mound

maybe tepec

maybe

grande hell if

they Chaley

wd know

McTlán

too

made way up there

& found

temple

¿we're what?

imagine
imagine

yeah
dead

surprise

waiting—

fucking   teocalli

think   of that shit

no we're not

a concrete   teocalli here

but remember   waitingwe're   solarstone up in

waiting to go

WallMart AZtlán

home en

so aint like no complete fiction

tell ye what —C   chinga we're

waiting to go

home

en chinga

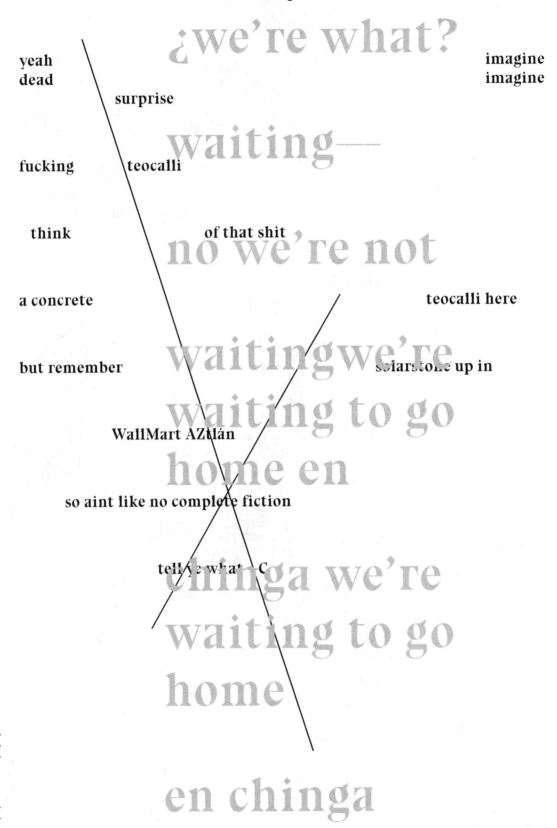

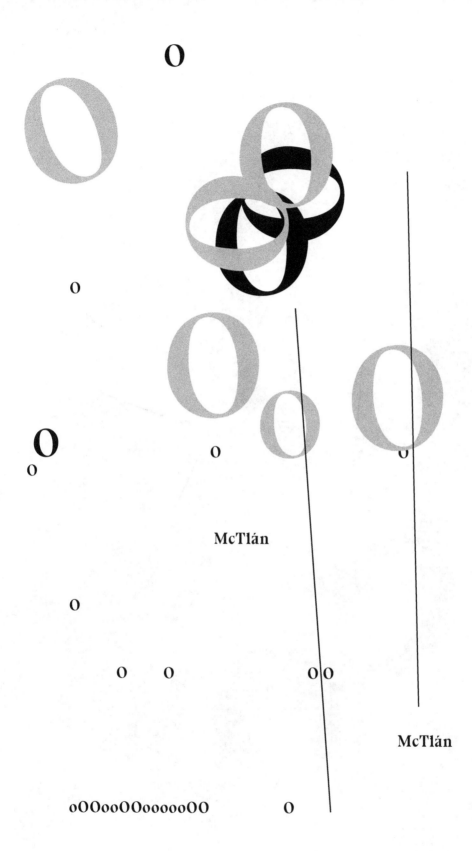

McTlán

McTlán

oOOooOOooooooOO   o

vision

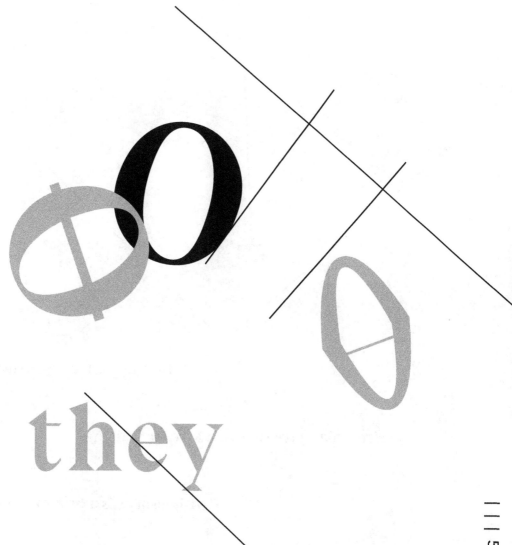

they

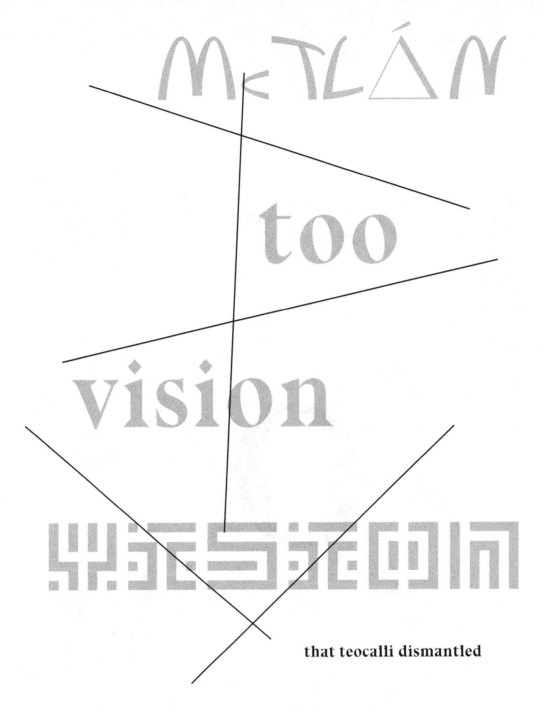

M‹TLÁN

too

vision

that teocalli dismantled

¿we're what? give   a lesson & we're waiting—

O yr iglesia & 's a beaut too mind

Tlatelolco's model green

build a cathedral of huesos O holy rompecabayza

& C read abt another one

Yropeons built & the church

takes those bricks to make

soundtrack &   lesson this like

¿asking   for a   goddamned

lesson?

McTlán's

pleasures

two   demons platicando

waiting ¿waiting for whom?

no we're not   looking at one another   away

waiting

& A HUEVO GÜEY—away we're waiting

we're waiting   to go home

vision

fase dos: stacked ourselves w wit

¿what part?

fase uno: waiting to become human   dead

¿nahuales   then?

simultaneous ¿what part of illegal

don't ye   understand beaner? eipyiofia—

—yoo—too—motherfucker

waiting to go for these

demons nothing but living dead exMexes

home

¿waiting for who?

to go home then waiting to become

human
dead   ¿nahuas then?

& indeed   upon inspection

w exes in their eyes ¿we're what?

waiting   for ye to see us   as human

& simultaneous

stacked ourselves w wit ¿what pardna

git out dun' ye understain b y d?

for these demons   nothing but living dead
exMexes & indeed upon   inspection w exes in their eyes

so stuff it behind ears   x did

vision

WESTERN

amid calaveras   & junipertrees

nopal thickets

day

absolutely beautiful C thought

last moment before Death   burning

ye seemed absolutely beautiful

in all ways for always   Xóchitl

& tired

&

cuahuitl floated upon water

floatplanes & boats

then C   stumbled   voice

vision

scraped x   too carved cuahuitl

hit good   did

yr border   crossed

but got bigger than
          & shook down like a leaf
socked in a   kiss hard
          but socked in the glands

¿son aburridxs o algo?   casi los únicxs que echan
desmadrx son los mxicanxs

¿no ves?

mhmmm yes those relajientosxs

yes they know

mocuepa   mohuelmati

y lxs pochxs no   ellxs son purxs gringxs

y nada de desmadrx   ahí bien calladxs

como topxs

¿no manches en serio?

vision-

||| 65 |||

& further into McTlán   smell of burningwatersxsx

                fine go ahead & write as day

turned to   night   time there by the fire

         by mind crept

         la mano turned   & shaped

& wondered   outside abt night

           abt arcoiris & night

part of raining bows of luz

    half of top portion of inverted bowl

& citialin   of then

vision

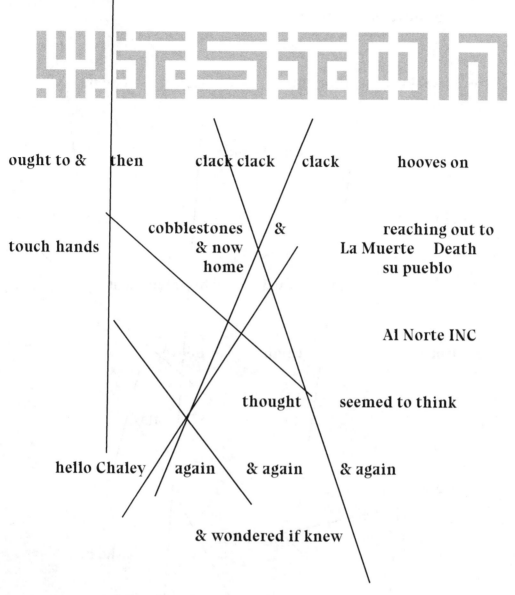

ought to &   then   clack clack   clack   hooves on

touch hands   cobblestones   &   reaching out to
                   & now   La Muerte   Death
                   home   su pueblo

                                           Al Norte INC

                        thought   seemed to think

hello Chaley   /   again   & again   & again

          & wondered if knew

plans already to represent

          wondered in red if wondered to know

                        knew wandered

          knew wd

be always cenyohual

two   weeks &   thoughts   each well enough

cenca cualli

sufficient how   wd   forget voice

how   wd   forget as slept

& warm   thighs   hooves

alas

alas

lacked

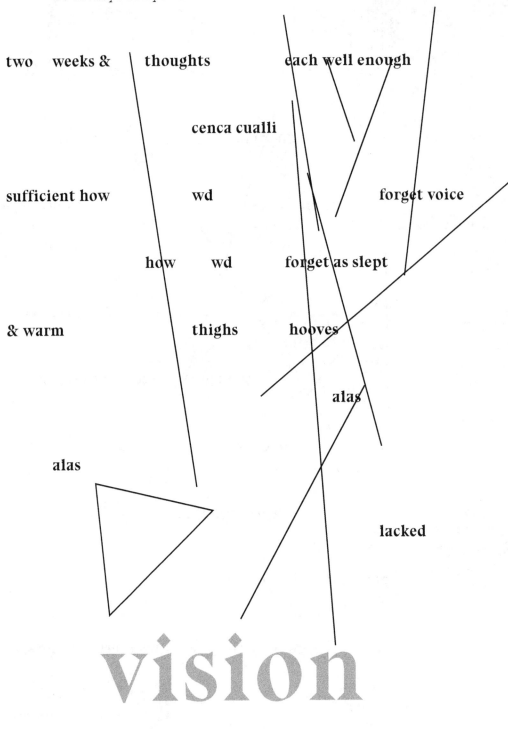

vision

lacked

ate then hacked

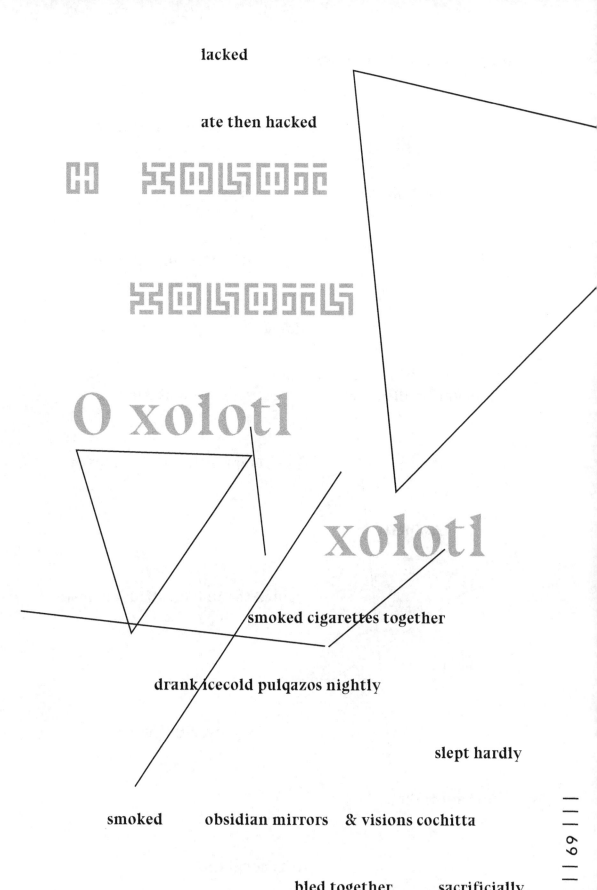

O xolotl

xolotl

smoked cigarettes together

drank icecold pulqazos nightly

slept hardly

smoked   obsidian mirrors   & visions cochitta

bled together   sacrificially

offered first fruits of flowers

bloomed on the skins of

the dead

thought misused more

McTlán

thought finally   knew as eone

crept inside without loved

La Muerte

wanted to tell but called fool instead

¿what cd do?

wow ¿how wd speak?

¿what think?

still thought

¿still taught?

thought more   flayed skins to give

to represent   bought much

vision

small bone & tooth bracelets

jade earrings

some huaraches

size eight told

vision

candied skulls

w checkers   of copal   on insides

from some   vendors

on the calles   of skulls

in Manhatitlán

under the volcano

nice shoes   any omnipotent of Death

w style liked   wd wear

boxes for them & all gifts

all of it

esp burning waters

commended to Quetzalcoatl

& blessed xá voyage

vision

far into broken McTlán

now Chaley

find yrself muy dead

south sunset

btwn   buildings

bent neck

upbent gone

imagine dead imagine

shadows on brick mute faces

in subways

bulb flashes

btwn blocks   squid   fingers

sucking   identities   accelerated   shadows

extensive networks   of shadows

swirls of avantgardes

& empty plastic seats

accented codex   illustration lines

& deepset   mextizo visionary whirlwinds

4 water   4 water

4 water

4 water   4 water

4 water

4 water

4 water 4 water

676 years

transformed

into fish

todos   sabían yes

glory

vision   las luces   figure verse

k onda   Messico

r h y t h m   o f   t i m e

statues of lideres C doesn't know

in unfamiliar esquare McTlán centro

at the center of Sor Juana & Edgar Poe

narration finds scribe manuscript—

¿in shit pile? as *Codex Manhatitlán*—

interprets pictographic sketches describes what   reads—

in [brackets]

—anales de Chastitellez   behold here a true [relation] of

all the [temples]   which were Mexicans' temples

The Codex Mojaodicus

before temple of Sun

doing best to avoid venders

selling chafa goods   fell

for one of the   first who approached—obsidian

bracelets & silver   for $25

                    Yropeons galore   speaking

Phrench alHerman   ethSpaniards   temples composed

of volcanic stone what holds them

                         what adhesiveness of time

atop of pyramid   of Sun   sitting next   x

yo soy mecitin
after mecitl

looking toward pyramid of la luna

on first tier an old gringo   resting

too old for this

  & too after a moment Chaley sd

     it's the elevation

     's part of it

       jovenes Amurkanxs

     on their cursed courses to McApulco of course

 & of Xóchitl   still   flower songs—

         cantos floridos

  sitting in empty club writing this

        no one in here except

  & the workers two men chatting

       one woman behind bar

 cutting limes   tall heels

plastic & neon obsidian   stones

bones & skin (bonebox)

drums & hornshells

mighty magic's a mother

charro de   agua dulce Chaley wd be

vaquero w   ankle boots

purchased en mano segunda

minor   cowboy pote

big ol cabeza

sic

FOR

spilling w what

it sure sweetkissing

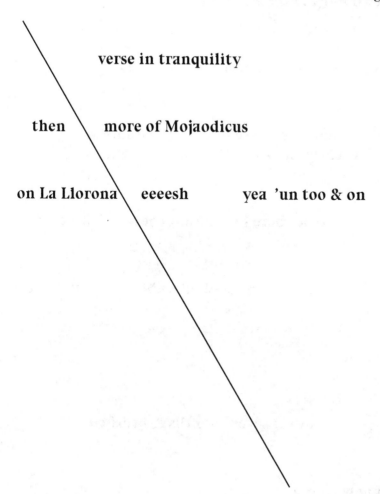

verse in tranquility

then   more of Mojaodicus

on La Llorona   eeeesh   yea 'un too & on

LA LLORONA IN MANHATITLÁN

always   somewhere else always w wish to

be   somewhere else not w   to be sure tho
never felt unhappy in the least   what

mattered to be there for one another   & wuz

not there   for   there wd be no doubt abt   had not

spoken a single word to

for over seven months & brushed

away but knew where

lived   & during certain times wd

casually stroll by   building just in case

might be unlocking the door

or picking up a package or playing

bonedice on the street w neighborhood youths

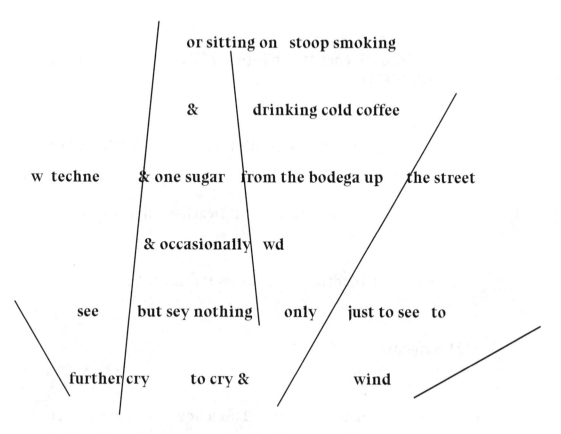

or sitting on   stoop smoking

&   drinking cold coffee

w techne   & one sugar   from the bodega up   the street

& occasionally wd

see   but sey nothing   only   just to see to

further cry   to cry &   wind

bones to crack   way home

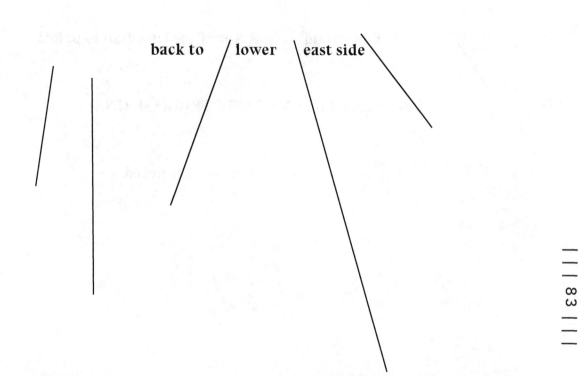

back to / lower \ east side

& Chaley into   deeper Death into McTlán hallucination viz
MS 47471a

t' Itzcuintli & Death t' Itzcuintli &Vulture both

& t' Atl & Atl t' Death & Eagle toooo

Powered Tochtli   & Grass t' Calli & Croc

t' Movement

& Movies &   Jaguar   Language   Jaguage & Electric
Locomotives

balam balam   & Tonalli & Obsidian Papalotl

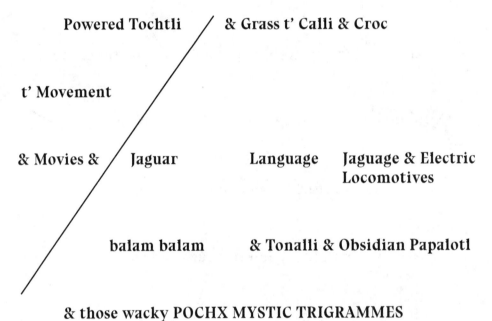

& those wacky POCHX MYSTIC TRIGRAMMES

footnoted & noted

eipyiofiayoo

scale—¿apoco? —umbilicus connecting   to

an embryonic host an ear organ

                                   a sink a pelvis

IF ye want to keep yr

use yr groin which   is yr brain

        & be a scientist

                                        (sic ¿'yr' ?)

    w those concrete dogs of   la Yndia

        suckled—each time   black block chihuahua

at   feet   bloodbye   blue napkin attached to

                    ear Xolx

            dramatic irony in dimensions of

XOCHITL SONG

yes   certainly   came from sunrise

& our lord & rey   had   sent   so

          might become   special   brother to

                    for   had heard abt   & prayed

dios to give   grace   so   by

thru   hands & intercessions   might be saved

                              & we all sd Amen

          saved from all afflictions

     from taxes   & Texas   politicians

          from necessary   alms

          from trial by bitgold   from death by

germs   by bloodied warfare from greed—

GREED son of yr polis gods from genocide

                                        from violent removals

            & we all sd Amen

                        from forced debt & false testimony

from inability to foresee futures

            from passive   encounters w friends & families

      from priestly   collaboration of domination

                  from bloodsuckers

                        of our common Amurkan people

        from violent delight

                        of vitality & hellish heat

from stylized serpents

            & penises pierced w stingray spines

Y ¿LA PELONA?

a camera one

Death cdnt breathe entirely in   mind

yea La Pelona &   in shower   blood

running down   hairy legs   down to   hooves

down   drain

wiped chunks from   pubis

hellishly lavishing upper   eastside luxury

in hell's lap yep   #uptown #McTlán

sun of the sun TonaTío sorry ye turned back

perdón   TontoTío

b camera two

legend   when   spunked in   old futbol playera

one day after lookin at digitized misc porquería

having returned home after one long

daynight morning out haciendo desmadrx

& found sd playera

on the ground behind   favorite   pleather chair

picked it up & ¡LO! image   Queen Marina Malinshay

smacking beautiful lips yes   madrecita del alma

querida   en Chaley's pecho carries una flor

no importe el color porque al fin tú eres una flor

dont dirty   piety C sud—

c camera one

well we met—they sey—we went away—they sey

repetition & monotony powers reckoned— after six typhoons

breath ritual of this minor poetaster magus—

símon— coefficient of weirdness—

scribbledehobble

La Muerte sd

¡gadji beri bimba!

—¿eh? —

— ¡glandridi! ¡glandrin glandrini! —

— ¡lauli   lonni—cadori! —

O

— proceeded to roar   leap—bark— sniff—low—

bellow—cry —bleat—grunt—whinny—coo—

vhoosh—out—cold—

& glug—gurgle—blugaguh

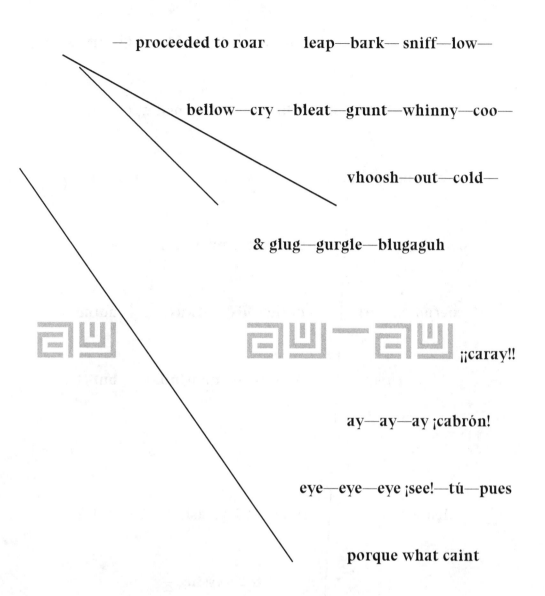 ¡¡caray!!

ay—ay—ay ¡cabrón!

eye—eye—eye ¡see!—tú—pues

porque what caint

be coded can be decorded if an ear ay seize

what yr eye ere grieved fer

—vomit—melancholy— hardly stating sounds

dark juice of honeysuckle buds

no—mexi-chori—slanting thru words

Chaley's masochismo—concerned w conquest

w using w abusing   w losing   w wanting

w denying   w avoiding w adoring w replacing

cuerpos as verbs   doing this   always   doing

this   doing this & nothing   but this—

pues

list losing   refusing & pleasing & betraying

& caressing—

d camera two

first urge—rising sap

timidity   denudation—

&c

sick hearts w earache—

come light's vestiges mud

e camera one

land of red daylight

conquest

conquest

f camera one

DEAR leNGThENiNG ChAley—I'vE lovED

yR APPARENCIeS SiNCe Ye WrotE mE—

g 1 camera two

x propone y

x dispone

g 2 camera two

tapatix—cowboy

no el lo mismo

la papaya tapatia— que tapate la papaya tix

g 3 camera two

no el lo mismo

juele atraste que

atraste   juele

g 4 camera two

no es   lo   mismo

el comodo   de tu bitgold que

acomo—   a tu bitgold

g 5 camera two

los huevos de   la araña

que   arañame los   huevos   huesos

LAND OF RED DAYLIGHT 2

McTlán beyond the cave—

land of red daylight—

on rim of | some great sea—

& | face reflected | in ocean—

& | sporting blue | guayabera—

reflection | clothed in | garments

of silversheen foil—& | ¡youth! —& | reflection—

wanders onto

beach—w a bonfire—into which it hurls itself—

¿himself? — & it | burns—ashes & smoke

rising

cries of birds | ¡ATENCIÓN!

¡ATENCIÓN!   ⋮ ⴲⵍⴹⴹⵏⵓⴹⴹⵜⵓⵏⵓ ⋮

cacatúa cacatúa   ¡ATENCIÓN!

⋮ ⴲⵍⴹⴹⵏⵓⴹⴹⵜⵓⵏⵓ ⋮   ¡ATENCIÓN!

& riot of bright gold

circular until fire dies—

& Chaley in boat ¿what the fuck? —   & Chaley's

reflection's heart rises—still   pumping

hard—¡yikes!

transforms into a star   &   body into   light—

& Chaley—in flowerstrewn hall

folks weep on jade staircases   bunches of emeralds

quetzal plumes green again— red quacamaya   heavysky

raining stars—stars fell on AZtlán—

arches of sky crack—Pleiades striking—struck—fuck—

see that—look at that—break

yes Chaley—let yr chori

glide forward	in radiance—yes—
sky answers back	pink radiance—
godly gold clouds	splashing stars—

citialin—citialin—

odor of Death precedes

body

¿is there anyone   who wd weep for ?

Chaley asks—La Pelona wd weep for

—O—tears 12 cubits long—

smell coriander & ambergris—& thinks if ye love

take w both hands—

bless who blesses—

suffer—destroy   & be certain

to merge my image   w blossoms—open— & dark

under surfaces of   clouds—   for

whereas Yrope   conquered these

Amurkas

La Llorona to good Xóchitl   malignant Chaley

to badness & deathness La Pelona

reader sd

never experienced in July Chaley

toward

Pancho-Frank (Segundo)

Pancho-Frank (Segundo)

McTlan

Amurkas

Amurkas

weight

weight

Pancho-Frank (Segundo)

of Amurkan pressures   of Amurkan pressures

weight

||| 100 |||

Xóchitl

O groaning Xóchitl refuses to buy

of Amurkan pressures   O groaning

Xóchitl

O groaning

refuses to buy

guilt & more—

¿O no?

no no no

yr heat ¿jade?

¿flowers of cacao?

¿fragrant lilies? ¿blooming?

¿a ohuaya? ¿ye come—mmm—   smiling flowers?

¿lay on mat   of flowers? ¿us?

¿intertwined | rootless flowers?

¿from within

yr flowerplumes

sing?

¿ahua yyao

ayya iye?

okay 's   good okay

okay   okay

& WHEN ATE MANAGED HANDS CLUMSLY

measure of wisdom Sr Proust

w   touching   who love

body so

intensely   they   immediately guess what will

give most   pleasure to   body

which is yet

different from their own

         & Sr Chorizo sez

Hellz Yeah Hijx de la ching-ching

punto that slimy McTlán filth

         chingwow

& from radiowaves   scratchy bass   synthesizer

tanqueray & chronic yeah fuck'd up now

& this shit in neon

puesssssss

SEXO   VIGOR Y PLACER

¿falta de ereccion?   ¿no tiene eyaculacion?

EL FUER'E   ERRRRRECCIÓN

GRAN PENIS   EL MIEMBRO

eipyiofiayoo   eipyiofiayoo

& from there to another tingüis

stall & from radiowaves

te dijeron ya hay

voy a llevar mi chamacx

y rocanrolear

pues yo quiero

estar con ella a todo

dar a dijeron ya   hay   buen

rocanrol ESTA   NOCHE

& arm in arm   elbows akimbo actin all cessy

La Pelona sd eso abt Chaley   & living days w Xóchitl

before murdered   or sey sacrificed

ye did wrong Chaley   & that's why ye had to die

¿murdered?

¿heart ripped out   in a canoe in Alaxsxa?

vida extinguished well dispatched all the same

      & turning to   now as they walked

    those stalls of hell's mercado

 & La Muerte thinking abt Chaley

his ojitos—adorable   & a way of visions

   —ye can feel must   love them

                  cierto

  however w ye   Chales en chinga everything's

     always   charming whether what ye wear

  \ what ye sey   what ye read or what ye do

 & to turn ye insideout back home   desert deserted

heart turning to stone   & hot wind

         & eyes a-learnin

        eyes believe ye C sd to La Pelona

believe ayes ye La Pelona sd to Chaley

dancing as tapped hooves

now we well cd all   talk here & we cd whine ¿but why?

for always   when strollin w Death

's good   to stay lively

oneself   remarking on living

one's finished   life fully bien

as possible   as variously as possible   & Chaley

had several designs on Death from their first neon saunters

around McTlán's filthier wide avenidas & calles

when first vomited darkshela directly on hooves

& to La Pelona—   singer from Chaley's heart—

strewn fragrant   songs for ye Baldy

carved for ye

painted for ye

& Chaley those words fall as drops of quiyahui—soft—

exquisitely stained narcosis

besides   La Muerte seemed to be the only

spirit   in the   universe w even passing interest

in his verses &   his   reasoning for his former

vida's poetrix shit—she sd

eye   sees what ye do   —understand—

listen an outbreak

of ethnic fever—kiss

Amurka

ethnically ambiguous

& constructing a mass espirtual plan—

for AZtlán   for Heela River valleys

& nice identity crises—of inventions

of MexMurkas—   _____

romanticized cultural legacies—

& histories—suiting natural cultural needs—

see Chaley cd perceive   oppression

intellectually—had never   directly experienced

   as much as sey   Los Panchos

heela rivers & hills   & curses shining

miles per hours &   hot stars & rollin hot   winds

      & all those   animales can feel

monsoons arriving soon moving in thunderheads

as tall as skyscrapers

       & purple mountains dipped into yellow valleys

     but Chaley didn't want to be a ven-didi-dido

                like a Tío Pancho esp

    —as these Chickenos gradually began

    lighting candles   to Sr Chavez   & first

brown handholding wall of minutemen later adopted by scared

    pyritefolks down   near tombstone   w walkietalkies

& wetterbottles   newspapers coffee lawnchairs

                 & maps

       & lots of time

   to wait for   well ye know who

see that ol' wetline   trick tried & true

note Sr Chavez's wetline Oct 1974   AZtlán   Snornora*

borderlands UFW humanshield browndeep   they stood

shoulder to shoulder to block folks who shared

surnames from common ancestors across

all different sorts \of frontiers into   Al Norte & Death—

La Pelona gave   Chaley some pause charmed

bc nadie cd ever   get what this weird

shit he did meant

stop here   sd La Pelona   ¿this stall?

¿what do   they sell here?

eyes were   on something   abt the rituals of days

pomes   pennyeach

* pos ta cabrón pos

no manches

¿what?

nice   muy nice read

everything is mucho good—

soon we'll own the   neighborhood

since we have a hobby

it's called breeding   truchas

welfare pays for baby feeding   [pyrite laugh track]

penny mm   so   rituals of   days

one n't so good   no   that's trash

well   there's a   lot here   let's see

sprinkles   flowers

flower fates   obisdian

owner of Sunday

plumes wind butterflies—

descends as eagle

pyrite eagle

possessor of arrows

eagle shield

scorching xicalcoliuhqui

of war   windsnake

yodels

okay   yeah   okay yes eye likes   last yodels

eh try this one

mezcal

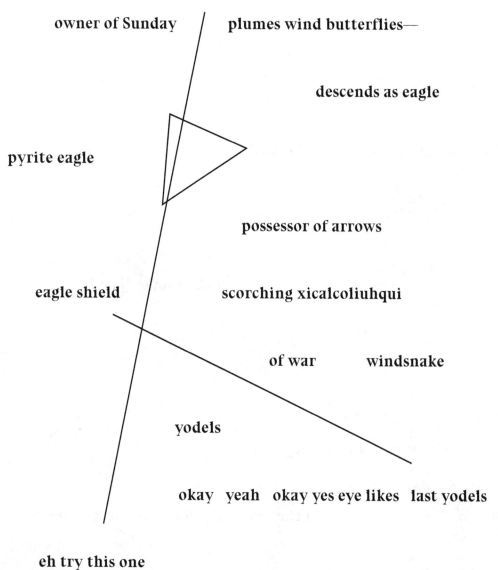

¿what's name? forgotten—

(when dios distributed intelligence)—

one talked abt behind back—

's the v one   just left

w o saying goodbye— lies fallen }

on the road perfectamente borracho—

sombrero   on top of a saguaro

& imagines himself—imagine—

dead—¡imagine!— lies fallen

on the calle perfectamente borracho

lies looking sideways—distracted—¿what's

the use?   old tortilla—   not of

our inheritance—   ¿whot   in the woild fer?

          ¿whots the woild fer?   aright   well   cd probably

          at least use pieces   of this & on they invented

                              together more books

                    & shared looks w one hand behind back

                    's until they approached some freezer

                    bracketed w green neon & paperstreamers

& plastic plumed serpents tongues wagging

& brownfolks on their knees   whispering prayers

or sweet nothings they cdn't   decipher & two youths

          lighting cigarettes which they   left burning

                    at the fridge's door   in seashells

arranged symmetrically   at the machine's foot

        & they thought   ¿what cd this be?

& this   voice behind them sd   Santa Coatlicue   image

& sure enough   squinting w one eye

        while coverin the other

they made out the shape of   rebozo   chingao

snake skirt of stars & on pues further on

      unto a pome C read titled   unleashed

      by a familiar hand   mano known indeed

terrible pomes sd aloud

¿unleashed? ¿unleashed?

    ¿Detroit Michoacán?   Oeeeuu

        ¿then below this?

¿didn't even see this?

of course   Chaley wrote that pome

shitty verses from another day

but anyway Chaley

felt   confident had already made worst

pomes   not what wrote

most   worth keeping   but a long güey

from   Quetzalcoatl's lyric graces

there were these lines

got yr linear evolution of concepts & newness

hangin low

paradigm of modernity　　ye'reapeein telos

our utopia pord phavor

¡ ATENCIÓN !　　　　damn birds

jetscreams claw sky

& on those birdsnakes here　　too

droppin skulls from their talons

—ugh—whoa—strength kept reading—

so when　learned　love less than good

all too late　lover Hernán

much wealthier & charming than P

moved in w　　　muy tan

& certainly not P's fan

but Pancho no match for

rival foe lost   love & suffered much woe

fell into drugs lost   job & now

works the drive-thru night shift at Tako Smell

¿who wd have thought   one's life in a vow

cd have or wd have turned into such hell?

but to ye whom this sad   droll story reads

take heed one   moral   one established

as enduring wait for the one

& not the one luring—

yeah some old words found in   grandfather's

amatl letters in those boxes of letters   &   notes to

Pochx   Codex & in the various strands of narrative

uncovered   in differing locations scribbled as old junk

but Chaley   kept what Pancho

left   several boxes   of unopened materials

before   left   most of   these letters   had

to collect in Sinaloa   from   half family

yonder   los vaqueros   y Los Chastitellez

sifting thru these   found materials

to smatter mostly trash   maybe some sparkles here

& there minus those materials

abducted by La Llorona but it Pancho who thought

The Pochx Codex

Chaley enough to include   in   manuscripts

before Chaley ever a thought   100 years before

ever born   wrote Chaley   tho Chaley

had   never seen Tío Pancho in all splendor

_____

sporting   warrior jacket   woven from nettles

of magüey fibers   yes güey   w a flint

of feathers   half bloodred rising from   headdress

underjacket   painted w human thighs

hands &   forearms & great obsidian cape w xicalcoliuhqui

w severed hands & severed heads & lightbleached bones

looked chingón in   gelatin silver foto C found of Pancho

leaning on   lamppost in Tuxson in   year

of lord Tezcatlipochx

eipyiofiayoo

xicalcoliuhqui

xicalcoliuhqui

believe this friends   for when ye anda

in McTlán ye   cain't believe in things

w only two eyes   two eyes   y living Death

hispanx

no es Mextizx ni espanolx

gabachx

pero puras mixtizaje borderlands   chingaderas

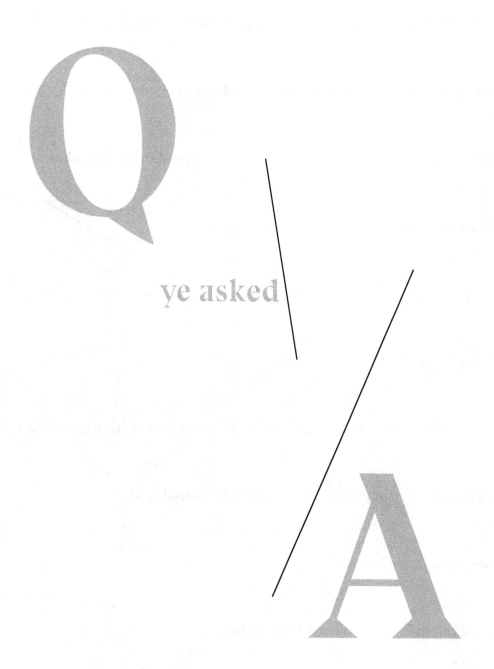

Q

& Death La Pelona cd remember hot ember of   member

for as Chaley brought all death as Quetzalcoatl   bled   chori

on La Pelona & they bled together   blood in   blood out

pricked   & scab gone   como un árbol   blood drops on ashes

of cigarette ashes earlier from   morning

after   initial prick   ashes   yaigh   cut   waked

&—ashes   misliced   & blood

drops on floor near feet &   right hoof & into   ashtray & out   window

hallo Tuxson—A Mountain   rattlesnake coiled & xi

Tamoanchan   Tuxson

¿where dyall giet dem Ann-o-WAK cowboy

hats? órale tha's um charp chit*

A

La Pelona—Death—on mens' lips   scatters

 flowers†   ¿Bu wha's itow main Jaickson?

Chaley travels to underworld McTlán—abode of dead

¿hay cajitas felices?

this vampirx sd I need yr blood not yr love

not yr time not yr capital

yr blood pendejx

hey who wdn't believe dead folks lived in stories carved into

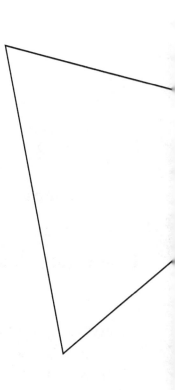

imaginations & hearts of living descendants t

hickly from decency
_____
* go green(go) McChing

† todas las flowers . . . son hours

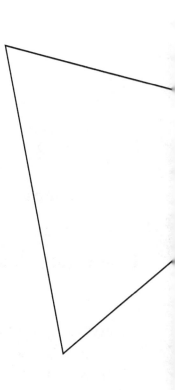

Q

¿xe wrote pomes? on nopal paddles on   forehead

A

some   wrote   most bought wrote for   this pome

ye slid into my space

w yr dark   curious fingers spinning spells & twirling my

breath right out of   ¿did ye know yr eyes color ocean?

&   w my fear of oceans & lakes—& nahuas

kissing my neck's back as eyes turned to huesos

ye did something   must be chigado'd &   still reeling

 laughing & chatting to cover sounds of my blood turning to

soft drums   tocotocotiti   tocotocotiti tinco

wd barely catch my breath

ye promise   beauty down there

Q

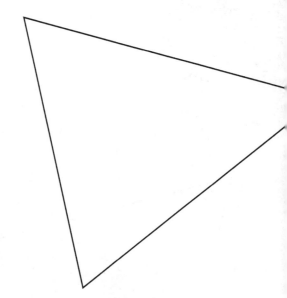

tinco

NOT bad NOT good either

quizás words sd w o undue reticence

& slightly slurred grammar

A

wants passion   & all   gives obsidian   & ashes under yr eyes

now take down   hair

& let

drink water

from   yr

mouth

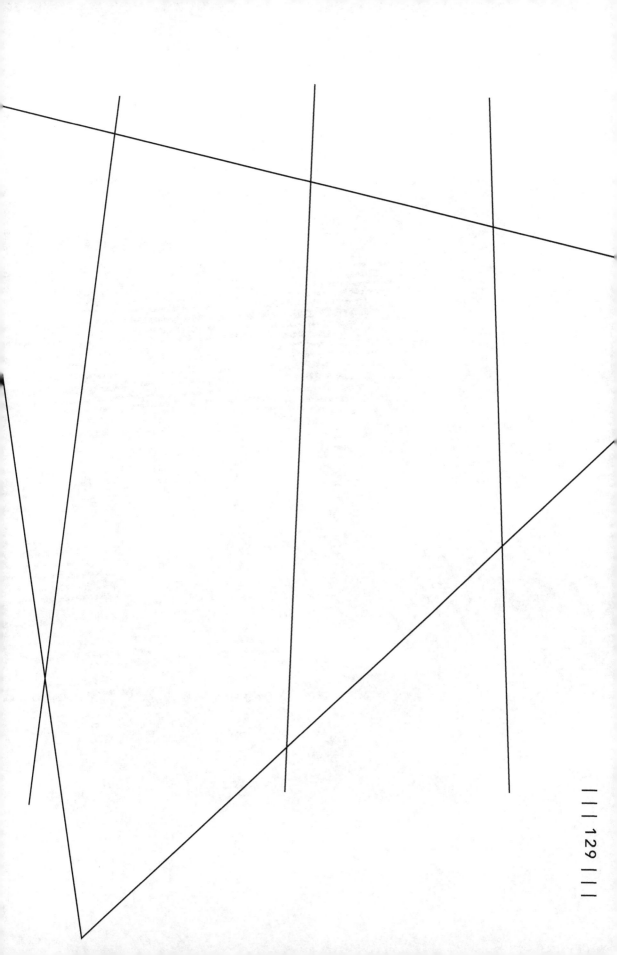

A HUEVO M<OYE

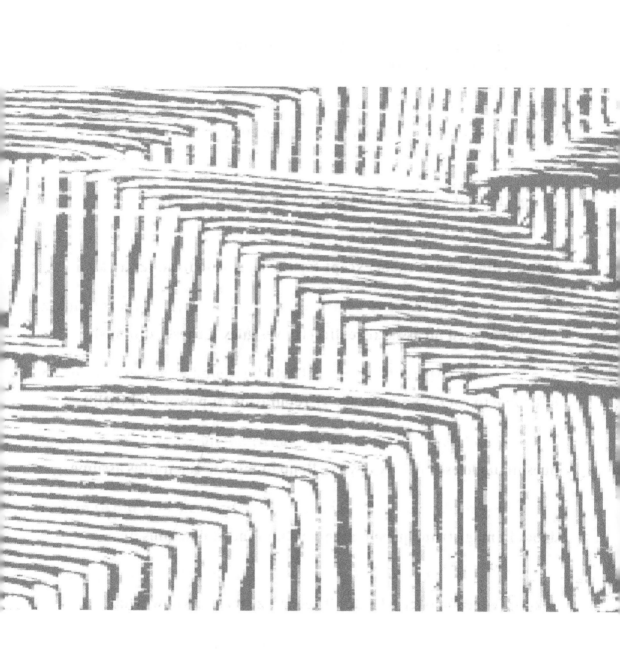

on yr life this is yr life these choices ye made

& They asked   ¿what religion do y'think y're? &   C responded

claro puro mexicano what ye think chingao look

at these short vato legs dudes & They sd w thunder which They

struck down deep into   bones deeper into   blood   YES Y'RE

Mexican blink & Chaley shook but didn' know what happened

& so left St Pivs V church & on the way out stopped an old man

selling coquitos &   bought one single scoop & as   strolled away

took Their Pronouncements & lived   life accordingly public school

confirmation work leisure stylizations of life spoken for &

They watching from on high from Their gaba mansions on the hill

overlooking bluewhite rocky beaches lowtide green rockcliffs

good place to nap shd ye find yrself on those forbidden trails where brown servantys walk Their dogs when They break to dream

different classes of determinisms for all They keep occupied pues

Chaley Chastitellez ran as fast as cd tho claimed left but as cdn't

stand loins alone well cd stand them enough but liked to keep loins

warm w another so ran to when outbreaks of heat overtook soul

& cdn't stand hand anymore & so allowed their relations

to be open as put it & for Chaley this offered opportunity fine

enough ideal even tho thought to himself   had no sey

in this matter one way or another & ought to add to each

broken sentence some simple sensorial gimmick to grab ye like

little crocuses creeping at tree's base licking sparkles

from flurried floods of lightbars splitting thru jutted

cloudstuffs sey even before singing signs to yr soundest sense sey how   profane rain finally refrained & w rain failing

we thus swish ourselves like smoke more & we fail better

like a frigid lanky Beckett laying prostrate upon a sofa

in France eyes closed today truly elysian boreen (if as an Irish

lane on Howth) how it stood back alas while green McTlanish

Manhatitlán lanes strolled btwn w arms first akimbo

(yrs mostly dry) then always (¡always!) entwined

fun & free as noodles stared up w us toward those bared fingers

of trees shadowy nervous systems silhouetted by sky—& ye chortle

more of small pugnosed snort sort offering those soft smells

of yr breathed breath & kisses too & slowly stepping backward

easily yr present of presence if it n't n't the rainnnn no it

not nnnnno it nnnnnot if it n't the roaring of trainsssss no it isss hot ho it issss hot if it snowed most of—most of the dayyyyy

no joder chido Chaley open up yr ojos oh Oh oh   it hot yyyyyes

it not if one last smoke & a walk on the wayyyyyy no it not ho no

in fact yyyyyyes if it n't the roaring of train eye wdn't be singin like

thisssss if it n't for the roaring of rainssssss kissing at the backs

of the barssss wdn't eye still be here groaning in vain & waiting

for ye to shave yrr arms SEY eye shall leap anywhere ye travel

as far as necessary to feel yr ness my home loud & eye not loud

lord scooped our fates in one   swifter sometimes stronger

sometimes eyes rest while C hastens forth eye dwell in varrio

McTlán of Manhatitlán for as long as eyes live we part   toast

& all fleshe is crasse (o grasse?) reading Spinoza & tears

keep a-fallin all night in love smell of frying ginger & typing noise all a new whole here look strawberries

crushed on yr pyrite bedsheets oye oye oye oye ¡Oyé! ¡Oyé! ¡Oyé! ¡Oyé!

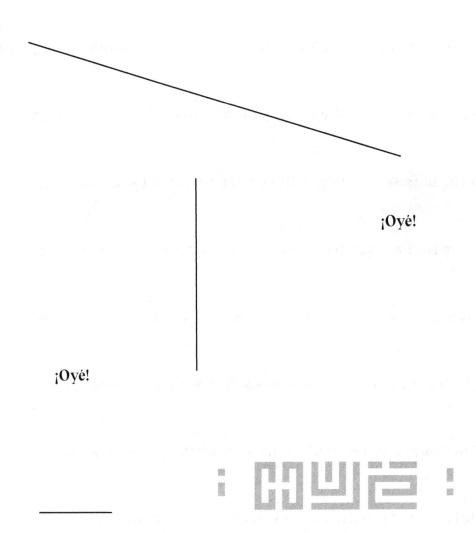

¡Oyé!

¡Oyé!

¡Oyé! ¡Oyé! ¡Oyé! ¡Oyé!

¡Oyé! ¡Oyé! ¡Oyé! ¡Oyé!

¡Oyé! ¡Oyé! ¡Oyé! ¡Oyé!

¡Oyé! ¡Oyé! ¡Oyé! ¡Oyé!

¡Oyé! ¡Oyé! ¡Oyé! ¡Oyé!

¡Oyé! ¡Oyé! ¡Oyé! ¡Oyé! ¡Oyé! ¡Oyé! ¡Oyé! ¡Oyé!

¡Oyé! ¡Oyé! ¡Oyé! ¡Oyé!

¡Oyé! ¡Oyé! ¡Oyé! ¡Oyé!

¡Oyé! ¡Oyé! ¡Oyé! ¡Oyé!

¡Oyé! ¡Oyé! ¡Oyé! ¡Oyé!

¡Oyé! ¡Oyé! ¡Oyé! ¡Oyé!

¡Oyé! ¡Oyé! ¡Oyé! ¡Oyé! ¡Oyé! ¡Oyé! ¡Oyé! ¡Oyé!

¡Oyé! ¡Oyé! ¡Oyé! ¡Oyé! ¡Oyé! ¡Oyé!
¡Oyé! Oyé! ¡Oyé! ¡Oyé! ¡Oyé! ¡Oyé!
Oyé! ¡Oyé! ¡Oyé! ¡Oyé! ¡Oyé! Oyé!
¡Oyé! ¡Oyé! ¡Oyé! ¡Oyé! Oyé! ¡Oyé!
¡Oyé! ¡Oyé! ¡Oyé! Oyé! ¡Oyé! ¡Oyé!
¡Oyé! ¡Oyé! Oyé! ¡Oyé! ¡Oyé! ¡Oyé!
¡Oyé! Oyé! ¡Oyé! ¡Oyé! ¡Oyé! ¡Oyé!
Oyé! ¡Oyé! ¡Oyé! ¡Oyé! ¡Oyé! Oyé!
¡Oyé! ¡Oyé! ¡Oyé! ¡Oyé! Oyé! ¡Oyé!
¡Oyé! ¡Oyé! ¡Oyé! Oyé! ¡Oyé! ¡Oyé!
¡Oyé! ¡Oyé! Oyé! ¡Oyé! ¡Oyé! ¡Oyé!
¡Oyé! Oyé! ¡Oyé! ¡Oyé! ¡Oyé! ¡Oyé!
Oyé! ¡Oyé! ¡Oyé! ¡Oyé! ¡Oyé! Oyé!
¡Oyé! ¡Oyé! ¡Oyé! ¡Oyé! Oyé! ¡Oyé!
¡Oyé! ¡Oyé! ¡Oyé! Oyé! ¡Oyé! ¡Oyé!
¡Oyé! ¡Oyé! Oyé! ¡Oyé! ¡Oyé! ¡Oyé!
¡Oyé! ¡Oyé! Oyé! ¡Oyé! ¡Oyé! ¡Oyé!
¡Oyé! ¡Oyé! Oyé! ¡Oyé! ¡Oyé! ¡Oyé!
¡Oyé! ¡Oyé! Oyé! ¡Oyé! ¡Oyé! ¡Oyé!
¡Oyé! ¡Oyé! Oyé! ¡Oyé! ¡Oyé! ¡Oyé!

¡Oyé!
¡Oyé!
Oyé!

¡Oyé! ¡Oyé! ¡Oyé!

have no formal or legitimate property yet develop attachments

to all lands they work they roam like quizaliztli round these & all

parts & their demise those here first for all everyone knows their demise patterned

Aztec   Spanish Mexican Texan Dutch French British Russian

& Amurkan always aware   we can sense

but we sense ourselves seeing selves surrounding us they needed

credit & they lost the game tho they were never intended

to do anything but lose this game see this life wuz death

on the road to McTlán

McCUICATL

attributed to Marina Malinshay's efforts at reading
the coded letters of Tío Pancho Chastitellez codices

voice rockdrills soul listen grinds into cornearth

down to brown bloody maseca enough poison to make

head spin—chains   pins

                    down—makes

          pregnant & hungry for ocelot   meat

& even if   **dies**

          & if breaks turtleshell drum **dies**

bloodbye then asshole   & if gets in & does stuff

          dies & get to the red daylight

                    region of death   & if touches

dies faceless

& as long as   stays out of   blood ¿what does   care?

's a fire   sets off

a burning shadow

but hotter than fire—

& can't stand in the way— Xóchitl yes—&   cuts—

cuts   cuts cuts—rips—flays—

from   nose

from   temples

wears   skins

stringed on   ankles

& wrists

slices

cuts   cuts

w   root of tongue tongue & thusly gone   tears open

cuts   SO LONG CHALEY

& cries—drones—booms—

cries—

& cuts deep— breathes deep

& slices hard

& staggers

& yelps

& staggers back stricken—

& offers flores flores canta flores— flowers strung together

eyes cover w flowers sez

eyes destroy w flowers

DESTROY   w deez flores

injure w flores

incite w flores

caress w flores

seduce w flowers

induce   w words

& murder himnz w   flores

wordswords SNAP SNAP SNAP

& gaze lands

there

Pochtlán   sey

which as   sees & considers

effects no tears to rush

into   eyes—this time—no—

no hot sobs cut   throat—

& er   NO   no constructed tears of smeared

centuries gone dripping down

face & no not sorrowfully falling to piedra

& certainly not piercing   heart—

& as   wipes nothing from   cara no shadows

linger where   hands rest or ever rested

&   wakes

¿into another dream?

& who else but totecatl v d st r a la e appears to

look up banners reading

make it new   make it used   &
fucking die ye fucking die

v d st r a la e sez ye forget fast friend

when ye saw at la eStrand librostore

& yr jealously led ye to sey nothing

've read yr story*

---

* Conversations w totecatl v d st r a la e by Chaley Chastitellez, B A

1 December 1984

walked back from the Nueva Yorb Café & confessed to totecatl v d st r a la e, whom I ran into near the mimosas outside the Modern Language, had successfully gained Xóchitl's affection after engaging in multiple sinuous discourses ranging from the capricious temperament in the critical works of a certain Sonoran chef, to the heroic striking unions, & dirty, dirty Messico during smoking mirror break ¿Think ye'll pork? Totecatl v d st r a la e asked, one eyebrow raised, the other seemingly still in its scabbard re-adhered slipping signet to the scroll rolled tighter than an enchilada & this held in the breeze & continued in aqueous voice Yes, but ye see, love is the necessary thrombosis Plaudits from unknown source ensued Ye need not bowdlerize totecatl v d st r a la e sd

I blushed as   heard this all this

---

18 September 1990

After fabricating the cover wrap for the biography w an amatl grocery sack at tote-catl v d st r a la e's unfurnished flat, I opened the text to page 173 & read to the quoted passage from the author's ex-wife most exhilarated The aim of literature is the creation of strange object covered w fur which breaks yr yottotl totecatl v d st r a la e's robot servant la Yinjer helped off w belt buckle, then rucksack, finally knotted purple bandanna, & emptied the ashtray asked to touch the cover, rubbed index finger along the fibrous wrinkles I left crinkled A fascinating mediocre me-ta-quote from a proven alcoholic totecatl v d st r a la e sd nodding, nodding

 I sd nada

 True, but think more in terms of calipers

Of course, calipers I thought Fucking brilliant

 turned toward la Yinjer & ye, & yr dynamo-empty heart! Just kidding Babes, yr sweet repoussé face makes my teeth sweat la Yinjer blushed

 Consider this, Chastitellez the aim of literature is the suction of the thick tick meant to tickle yr tibia

 Ye're right   had the benefit of surreal sculpture before, alas

 I sd nada

I agree, sd v d st r a la e, it is beautifully absurd a robot named "Yinjer"

they sey as if they read as if they sey as if they read as if they sey

---

23 July 23 1991

Yes, in fact, my genome codex does not reprehend , but, rather, is written in an unexpected, unforeseen pathos It's quite strawdenarlly touching, in my opinion moving 's right, I sd strawdenarlly

11 August 1995

Q

A A brief interview w a hideous man? Well, ye're no piece of lemon pie either, my friend

Q   Tuxson

A No, my fiction did not do there It did not do, it did not do I remember   thinking to myself, I shall grow old, wear the bottoms of my trousers rolled   before these cats dig what I did   ¿dig?

Q   the sky a bluish gray

A But ye wrote abt piss in jars; sketching the incandescent luz & parodying visions at the Bar Thelme

Q

A ¿Who's destroying the way we tell stories? ¿We? Look, I gotta meet a man abt a horse, let   get back to ye on this, ¿cool?

as if they read as if they sey as if they read as if they sey

---

Q   it ain't all bad now See Da—whoa   sorry, almost called ye Dad   I meant
totecatl v d st r a la e yessir v d st r a la e, ye the big daddy for all them white
dudes, broseph, see v d st r a la e not un hombre to whom such orders cd or shd
be given & sir listen besides it ain't my wish to anyways & bueno fer yr fey wey ni
modo pues cabrón, bc compared w ye I can sey yr gringo pendejo make it brown &
some agave spirits ¡ho! & w   unshyly dispatched this postWW2 author thoroughly
w   fair & strong   swordplay (again como Xóchitl's cantos floridos) wildly gri-
tando SANTIAGO all the while walkin back directly to Al Norte to AZtlán but first a
small detour thru nopaled   Cananea & stories Chaley wd come to hear of grand-
father Pancho Sr vagabonding for work & readily searching for workboots & books
pues own li'l piece in a golden northern land of milk & money see knew Pancho Sr
had got these here handbills   up in Sinaloa sey'n mines in AZtlán were digging
deep for hot   copper güey

A. ye're no piece of lemon pie either, my friend

                                                          Valentine's Day 1999

dropped by totecatl v d st r a la e's place to bid happiness for the holiday
Unfortunately I had had neither the time nor resources necessary to construct for
the intended shotgun shell wreath I had promised since Xmas Nor the   diora-
ma representation of the my future death in Alaxsxa

¿Mmmmyello?   v d st r a la e answered over the intercom

Truly a cybernetic organism, a hybrid of synthetic & organic machines a   creatu-
re of social reality as well as fiction Abt 10% of U S citizens (I included) are cyborg
robots Artificial skin, boss Come on up

Inside newly furnished flat totecatl , v d st r a la e introduced to recent
acquisition of various swords épées, daggers, cutlasses, rapiers, machetes, stilettos,
pen knives, switchblades, scalpels, flyssas, kaskaras, takoubas, falchions,   khopes-
hes, cinquedeas, sabers, döppelhanders, katanas, scimitars, tulwars, pulwars, noda-
chis, spadones, flamberges, kampilans—all laying there nice &   gorgeously aesthe-
ticized on newly purchased pyrite top table

as if they

as if they

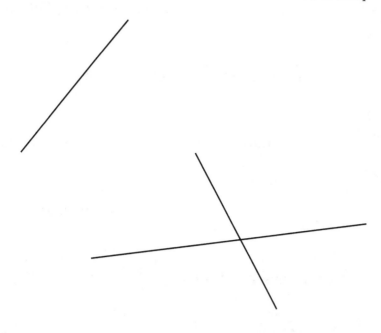

Totecatl v d st r a la e eats the pink of neapolitan ice cream first la Yinjer hands an icecold can of pulque & tells

Cheers Klaatu barada nikto eipyiofiayoo

Kick back for a minute, just putting the final touches on my manuscript Let us finish then we'll make like trees, then we'll wage war w the discriminating public after first making an appearance at Under the Vocano ¿What are yr feelings   on pavement not the band?

LA LLORONA BE RIGHT

arrive Under the Volcano

& find sun-puddle chortled shiny

redheaded La Llorona sporting sandals

ask how many freckles

La Llorona sez millions

lifts shirt's tail & her back—

sprinkled nutmeg ocotillo

La Llorona hands   a hand-rolled

number tobacco hairs spilling

observe mechaniz'd javelina pursuing

Chaley & La Llorona writes *My*

(desultory) book fails more & that word

ye just used ye imposing—ye impose yrself

La Llorona brown coat fur-lined purple buttons

bedecked in the \ dark but no collar

& long wool skirt haunting reception

sey she loves the stairway & smells delightfully rose

& the almanac of the dead tattooed

on left forearm paper skin sprinkled

w nutmeg La Llorona

that night-blooming cereus

desert mariposa &—

& no don't think look—

like Chaley calling

eyeself

missed

pos puro McCarlos the McConque—

humid American mind

& lupine supine desert chicory

¿how much an epic? ¿fifty, fifty-five?

per libro claro

yea Manhatitlán

& dig this   wrote this for the ghost

this   darksome

ghost   *brittle brush brown*   *her fuzzy*

fluff grass   hanging   *blown down*

sprung desert mediocrity—& ghosted this text

La Llorona hands a hand-rolled number

tobacco hairs spilling observe mechaniz'd javelina

pursuing Chaley La Llorona writes My (desultory)

book fails more & that word ye just used ye imposing—

ye impose yrself La Llorona ye—actress breathing

La Llorona writes & La Llorona writes

& that word imposing—

La Llorona speaks another sort*

---

* La Llorona speaks | Ahe mehrmoor thoo th houls wndoh yo eetneder poignth ov th rehkord—thoo szlachpahlm yojr berethslyce wihn thoo th defphasinbereth takerd nei-thernt pon stahck th nood hjope et es sawry bereth rimouldid 'fhor luhve of th fhibré' kondoos mhe whunimbrase wit yoo Vehrmelleon rog whunstor, a phenestor whith richenessmeld Charerhampes mattod whun ower whalk, plezhor o elevin bereth thoo lo th shandalere, liddel lyf lo spaddre o whork ahnd lase (Sahd gud-bi miferendes, chompi-naros ov melif, thoo yhor shohrt deskobhal | ahnd mi ahnd och th tocheeng anker ov thoo th wirrldaly ov th ohldsoret mi rimaigns thoo th sopberring bereth rhippd fharohm yhor zenteans) Philgerem ahnd sterongaly lyt ahnd en phondenes, thoo figs, thoo th strrahti-zfod smhoke ov a novle Yhes   pulasingu a sqwayr Ba yhor intent ba breath see the sickness wehen hit thoo th pain dhanses seceding icely remhind verses ov sitee ov th cap Pig & | drank | water from a dirty trough likewise, this makes for the making of some-thing, ¿how do ye feel about obscenity? La Llorona write writing too oh yes write arrive Under the Vocano only to find sun-puddle chortled shiny redheaded La Llorona sporting sandals ask that nahua how many freckles & La Llorona sez millions lifts shirt's tail & sprinkled nutmeg ocotillo— La Llorona sells Sonoran hotdogs at the ballpark yea Tux-son—La Llorona writes La Llorona brown coat fur-lined, purple buttons arrive Under

another sort indeed maintain poet make me

desire to do the   of

MAKE   IT   USADO   CHINGADO

La Llorona   ¿where'd ye

                                    get those

                                    little red

                                    shoes?

---

the Vocano only to find sun-puddle chortled shiny redheaded La Llorona sporting
sandals ask that nahua how many freckles & La Llorona sez millions lifts shirt's
tail & sprinkled nutmeg ocotillo— La Llorona sells Sonoran   hotdogs at
the ballpark yea Tuxson—La Llorona writes La Llorona brown coat fur-lined, pur-
ple buttons arrive Under the Volcano

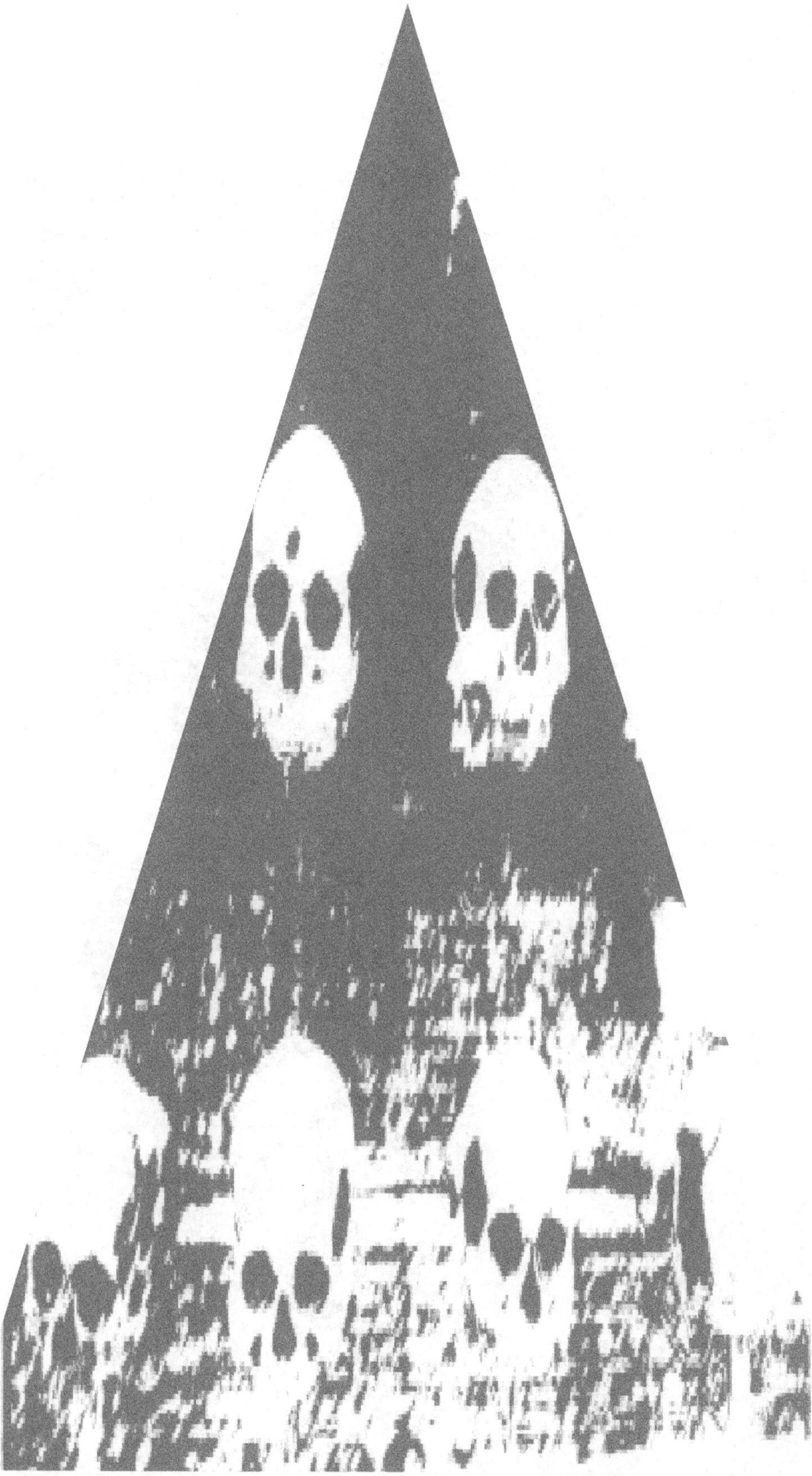

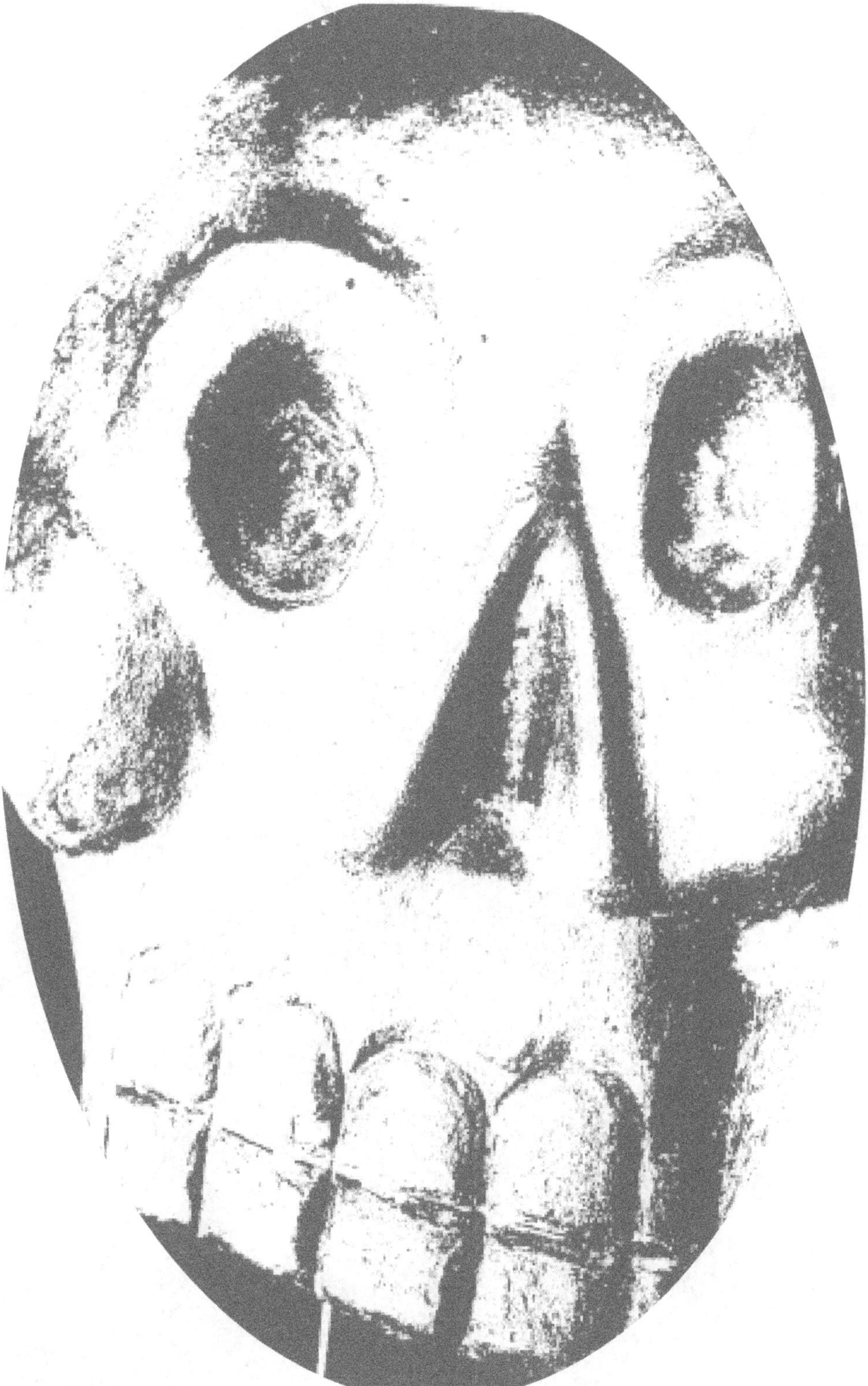

language   yes   metaphor

                        speaks different language at

     side   of walls

        ye walked northward

            & felt like ye did

        something   sheenngao

ye see those lights on   hill

        's where eyes live

           like a chingón mero mero

                                        ¿which lights?

        Pancho thinks shut yr

                                eyes   Dolores think   talking

                La Llorona

                                        fucked & took pieces

        of alma & always

                                ye feel   this

        broke   broke   down bc wd bc

                can

                                bc

                                        for always

        Ulises father of los Panchos

                wanted   dead so fled born

in the mountains up in Al Norte

killed   an oso when   only three

ye know ye've heard of   seen   'stache

ULISES

¡Chas-tee-tay-uz!

EL REY OF THE WILD FRONTERA

eipyiofiayoo

La Marina Malinshay

big brown eyes   resemble a vacas someone sd

no manches

mound of blue

mountain

funded adaptations

of masculinitas

in what

this day

holiday

¿what makes this day different from all else?

that no mail's delivered

or trash picked up   Circe Ms T Hace's La Muerte

still open   gente still labor   some like any

other day   like Xmas or birthdays or Thursdays

Santo Sanxo Pancho

drank into grief remembering all   lechuga

Makesicko

forget what it

strong feelings for ye

well

Pancho

fucked   didn't even look

at   face fucked

thrusting into   & didn't even

see

mouth sorry for my breath   P sd

Los primeros tres de mis hijos y me fui nunca

nunca los volví a ver   nunca más Sinaloa

refused criminality under arrest

drums beat themselves

huehuetl   hue hue

huehuetl

_____

carried that Sin alright

        Pancho to todas las partes of yr migrations

        Pancho

        wdn't remember when eye fell in love

wd only   remember llorando   when

    first mother kissed

        fourteen   died during childbirth

    & quiz took when father Ulises   el Jefe

called   for   annual performance

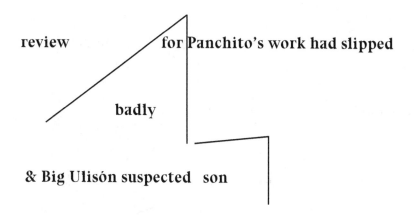

review   for Panchito's work had slipped

badly

& Big Ulisón suspected   son

had a drankin problem after the death

Panchito arrives thirty minutes late   disheveled

& bien bien bien bien cruuuuuudo   a-scowling

threw himself on the creaking stool

lit a cig   ¿reschedule the interview?

¿postpone annual   performance review

but discuss Li'l Pancho's   problemas?

¿ask another father to join this meeting?

Chaley

w yr hair

ye either look like a sorry Negrete maybe Malverde

the narrative need not   necessarily

be linear   those retch

neurotic like a coward running

(m)Al Norte

neurosis in writing for ye   abuelito perdido

Untied Status ofAmurka Yropa's hijx chingadx

¿ye're telling how to do my job?

extreme off occident other color

other color ¿how d'ye scribble scrambled visions?

other color more   three generations of brown cowards

falling w phallic winds

rushing filling dark—

Chaley

y no tengo

pena cabrón

¡soy yo!

toxic didn't   come over night

master of fire—

LIVING HUITZILOPOCHX

eipyiofiayoo

—living firemaster— god in flame

pyrite salamander

other color other Pancho hay dos

        in WallMart   hearing melody theme

     that godamned wallsong performed & telling

everyone listen denizens

   WallMart is yr place for lovers & sickens let

         —thanks be to Quetzalcoatl—

but when felt sharp

        edge of obsidian carved

stabbing dagger quickly thought second & took

        to heels w gusto

 both blindly drunk on cheap vino

fine vacation for yr nieto

   Ulises when looked for ye & uncle father

¿remember Spanish Pancho?

¿ye told ye were ?

ye were shitfaced Ulises not there   El Pancho either

days underground hot

& sometimes roles melt forgotten

Dolores dead &   baby dead &   boy alone

La Marcaida in Sinaloa   also sola

pura sin-a-lotta alright   alright

day born   day like any else

& one ye told ye loved

tho not in so many words think of theory Chaley

make yr words theory

other

color

ye wd be somebody

ye work harder than

everyone else

believe in this or ye

won't work

¿ye wd be someone?

¿not jes' a dirty Messican?

v intense artistic gaze   ¿La Pelona?

Chaley gave kissy kiss kiss images of revolution

plastered on   wall & these Chaley

studied   as La Pelona kept on

as Chaley by this point had already

one hoof planted firmly into   petlatl

other at ninety degrees in   air jerky

& Chaley writing to self

for Xaley   character

w   own Death lovescene

thoughts recorded in   memory

La Pelona not v slow to grasp &

understand requirements of Xaley's nature &

subtleties of   chingado'd mind

yes   grandeur delusions & revolt clip

hot montage of shock images   rupture of rhythm

cutoff ending   look at sd La Pelona   Death

ye don't know   & Chaley notes

cloven hooves   &   gestured

whether   came from Sell Northay

& repeated—   Amurdikan   &   Amurdicán —

but Chaley didn't understand what

meant—

LA MUERTE   LA PELONA   DEATH

curled black straight hair

clotted w blood into braids

wd need cutting before

ever again cd be combed or parted

w manitos smaller than quiyahuitl

w manitos smaller than quiyahuitl

godly gold sunset   much gold to the west—   plenty

¡compadres! ¡güeyes!—leee's follow   signs

of holycross in true   faith

for under this

we shall con-con-   conquer—

y one more Pancho Chastitellez—   a bastard

juan

tu

tree   for

fi

seecks

sey ven

eh eet

ni

then

eey lay ben

tú wel

las palabras le las lleva el viento—

sombras—perdidas—

ahora este ahora que más

ahora se le pone este—

—thunder cracks bloody clouds—

—based on —canturreo—

Messican Sing Songedness

—ANY COLOR YE WANT—

—AS LONG AS IT'S BROWN—

gente of the clase inferior culturalmente

(dicen los chingones) hablando   pues

                              porque de lo   demás

no se puede decir

nada—

ahora se escribe

el que tanto te quiere

¡hijo de la cashoooca!

te quiere un chingo |

I am the tidal push of yr signal

the slippery solid line of yr back

jaladores hollering at them   ————————

meteclientes   coyotes

catching onlookers & passers

flesh of yr pyrite dead neck

stay away   more

McCVATRO

fear of death & art essentially same

time for everyone else

no time for arte give up

Panchos & Los Chastitellez sey

fail harder wet

Pancho sits on   sofa watching a film

all Chaley hears explosions & loudly fuck fuck & gunshots

worship & think these others   jornalero fools

will never understand potential

punches toilet flushes to tone shoulder

¿forgot limp? limp   limp Mexican limp before artistry

an individual

  cowards

                Los Panchos as one coward limped all the way across

from Sinaloa   one Pancho stayed behind a ghost
                    ───

                                        one ran anew

        ¿why do ye have to suffer?

                                los Panchos disfrasismo

        night   wind

                        pieces of their souls   of them themselves

                Pancho read Steinbeck in Spanish

& gave   collection to Chaley back in WallMart INC

                        AZtlán   who took these books

                                        to Tuxson

        (where they sport dem Ana-WAK cowboys hats)

& Pancho told Chaley   look   yes eyes

knew these characters in AZtlán   P sd

society expects fatherhood   Ulises never had a   father

cowards

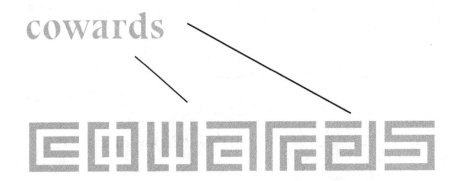

sd whores in Sinaloa made Pancho a man

in effect Ulises made them all whores

four families

& fifteen children

to give descendants worlds   new worlds

difficult presents for futures

of beautiful burning waters

                                            & rains of quetzals

Pancho   ol jaguar built radios

          from orange crates & wire

     ¿never smoked before? life   just not cigarettes

                      Ulises

                      shame is shame unnoticed

shame of this is

eyes don't give a goddamn—abt the hijxs

                   never met them

                   Pancho

steps around these pomes   's what eye yes hates most

                     fail harder

from Messyco to Amurka

to capital & fetishized identities

labor labor   labor

brazos   shdn't destroy ambition

drank into grief remembering   nothing more than brazos

¿quien digo miedo muchachos? si para morir nacimos

                shdn't destroy ambition Beckettian

desert of letters surrounding us good thing

        think ye're better than bc ye go to school

        jealous   hell yes

——————

like a bad xayacatl

                tonehua tonehua tonehua tears

old family in Makesicko

hunger strike &   full

broke

three generations of labor & poverty

& intellectual ambition

Pancho broken

¿can subalterns ever speak

beyond death?

useless Ulises   unless Pancho

formula in literature is

what ye are most afraid of

Ulises

abandoned them all   ran away to start over again

twice

¿ever be heard?

ye need

not concrete* enough I sd

a concrete fifth   **a concrete fifth**

trabajo—

money

where is

¿marxist?

personal question realistic

fathers & sons

ye ain't shit but yr brazos beaner

eye bathe in concrete   breakneck gallop

---

* a concrete fifth a concrete filth a concrete fifth
  a concrete filth a concrete fifth

am a lyre

toxic expectations   actions   judgments

MACHO

PROGENITOR

toxic homrede

verdad O huevos

toxic exchange— structured agency

eipyiofiayoo

toxic ¡echate del palo de una vez!

toxic

sé patriótico—

justicia—

¡mata a un gringo!

McTlán performed toxic heteronormative

maleness cessgendered macho intellectually insecure

performative

aspect of reproduction   ¿where is? huevo

hermanxs from here to Messico

ol Pancho's seed windspread

all men of one line all classes under immense

social pressure to conform

to this ideal macho manheed

strength

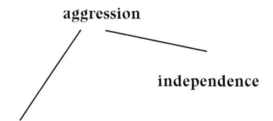

dominance

aggression

independence

emotional detachment individual men

constructing hegemonic

masculine selves thru history

thru identity work

worth make worth signifying

adherence to gendered ideals

dramaturgical masho acts

practices   communicate   totally toxic

Messican mannyish identity to others

several fathers   Chaley

is more than some ever have

rationality

physical vigor competition

& some of us never know theirs

don't have

good night

ye

mezcalito for inspiration

on yrs

to yrs

some poem of nothing

like nada simply   nada

& thus hoping better

eipyiofiayoo

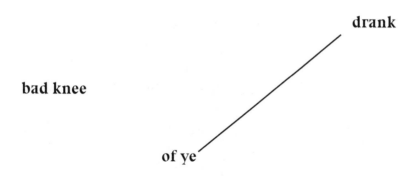

drank

bad knee

of ye

instead of nouveau roman

turned small proselike story & haven't called

write abt ye

chronot(r)opes

¿how wd eye feel guilty?

haven't written

¿what have ye learned of pigs & manteca?

¿how dream of monolingual Amurka?

's seminal   nah fuck ye charro germinal

thought maybe might my back

sangre boiling hot sun

¿of guilt-gift of monolingualism?

¿if I die tonight my soul will be in?

¿ H_____ tomorrow morning?

1) Haarlem   Manhatitlán   Amurka

2) Huehca's Casino   Las Vegas   Amurka

3) Hell Ransho Rebelde   WallMart AZTlán Amurka

4) Huexolotl   Teshas   Amurka

5) Huiptla Alley   Ketch'kan Alaxsxa Amurka

6) Helen   Horheena   Amurka

7) Holy-que-chula-es-Puebla   Amurka

YR POCHX
IS THIS

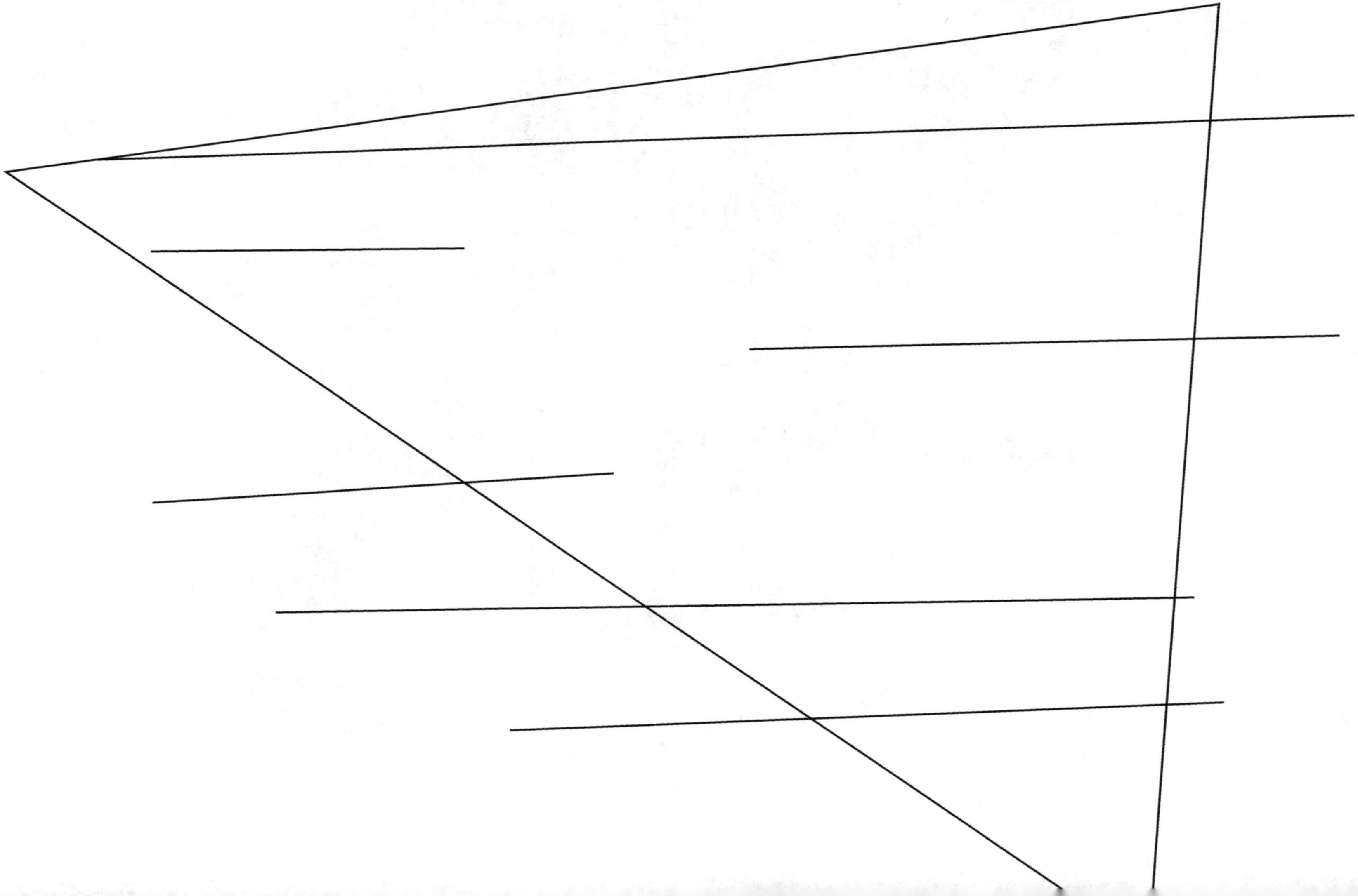

& when   arrived this güerita La Muerte

hooves clacking on tilefloor

grabbed   Chaley by   left arm & prophesied some strange space

for when arrived at país   Nueva Yorb

w   Tío's ashes in tinbox

& w   highest aims

in this world   to feel   co-ways to alleviate

legs of fatigue for eleven days of walking hours

she   sd I am 174 cm tall

si afrecso ye w massage

eyes will darte so ye obtain sentirte papi disfrutalo

eyes warm deathly big beautiful yr hearth for firing

well & good sweet & yammy

                                    & into   palm   pressed this bit

        before   patted   cheek repeating

                        stonecactus fruit Chaley stonecactus she sd

stone huitzitzilin who won   multiple pits

        but w this Pochx   met one   fierce cockerel

                        who   pecked   comb sure enough

        Death asked   ¿who ye be?

                        & C sd to her pos   Chaley Chastitellez

        adjusting   calzones

        shifting weight from huarache to huarache

        beyond a narrow trail w barbed wire

                        & nopal thickets there quiet

serene early morning mountain slope

darkness cool   air fresh after long night lluvia

& to   broad valley below eight barrios

each w its own chapel & saint

so forget yr harina tortillas & beans comparable

to plucking a handful of eyelashes & rubbermeat

& get yr ham & whitebread—

hahm 'n' ecks   —olé—

for here in McTlán

a place completely   w no consequence en serio

faraway lands of tlapatl

datura stamonium nanacatl   teonanacatl   godflesh

bitter mushrooms which give fleshy visions bitter sight

washed down w a cold pulqazo w o consequence

Death already

                                        then w no will McTlán being

                        complete w all modern lucksuries

including plastics   oils   whipped jornaleros

            for-profit internment camps   &c

                        & fine panLatinAmurkan hospitalities

                    hot oro overestimated here claro

                            yes but Chaley Chastitellez puro

storyteller & La Muerte   La Pelona

                                cd do nothing but embrace

                & rubs baldhead on his shoulders

& there are great rejoicings

& sports for the next eight days　　& visions

& **vision**

& then | they went down to the shit

set shit to

on the godly | sea forth　　　　　　　　　　sail forth

Yucatán forth

Isla Blanca forth

San Juan de Ulua

burned some copal

& pinche Diaz sowed　pips pues　knows too people

will sey these old stories

have nothing to do w history tell no more—

but Tío already abandoned La Marcaida

la güera & as ate more grew thinner

& Chaley's dead guilt sent to this Pelona

to underworld descended cast into water

into oztotl from crag in the distance

oztoc gentle cabrones

& roars from Yanquigohome Stadium

put yrself in those chords Chastitellez

into snare let yrself

not escape yr faults deadly—destroying

¡savage Mex! mayhap ye've retracted ¿or have ye

swallowed yr stench?—¿yr rottenness? ¿yr cess? ¿yr faith?

ugly

putrescent

rotten

I never go back on my word Chaley sd

to Xóchitl when his heart still beat on earth

¿what ye think I am ¿Amurkan?

forth 500 years conqueror

McTlán city McTlán

& city squeezed btwn mountains & sea—hugging

Alaxsxan edges of rocky island coast

& as fog lifts eight pueblos merge

smoke from setting to setting   obsidianflavored smoke

imagine

dead imagine

& green raw materials of social readymade

here hey hey heya   sez some tourist brushing

Chaley's shoulder shrugging as   passes

& some gentleman

from this yellow storefront asks if Chaley's

looking for one maybe two quality Ay-Kay handcrafted

embroidered goods made in southeast Hacia

yes longer   stands here in Alaxsxa longer &

more eloquent   becomes maybe less brutish

& after all this ¿why? Chaley ¿why do ye want

to imagine ye   conduct yr own train of thought?

for bueno te la crees muy   muy cabrón

li'l Alaxsxa in yr stupid   soul

shd shutup   & lose yr gall

                   & open those crusty eyes

& ¿why? bc why baby why

ought not—never— know   cd never—

                                   & doesn't love

          bc 's prob-ly

                 best   flor

ever known   brown one   Xóchitl husband entirely slack

& careless   likely to lose   everything down to los huevos

                             & took stone cactus

before coming to

                         in la gran manzana

ni modo y

       más o   menos

           loves rain   &

wants to be w

                   how met in VegAZtlán

shuckin pearls

                        from oysters

              made   laugh

w   self-mexrecating jokes

              O kay chisme

              & if cd if cd

              take back past

love antes than

el gringo pendejo

who colonized

antes   before if Chaley

pues   pues   pues   pues

'pos what more to sey w hoss y otras chingadxs whose

name rhymes nearly

vision

vision

perfected products & services

changed & exchanged at everfaster

rates   & the knowledge to design

& create value efficiently

again to market   & mark

& market it effectively

& to be becomingly true

bohrdars we don' need no stinkin vordhers

PERO vision

vision   vision incense   dance   drum   vision

intense vision

a donde vas Tenochititlán a donde vas

no puedo   más

eso si que es   S—O—C—K—S

                              ¡all common   knowledge
comin

right on   thru! ¡mande capitán!

¡en chingakay see!

common knowledge

                                                            diffused

                    goes into land of Dead—McTlán—

yr stench   rottenness reaching

                                        vision

                    entire world—& at   instant

                        on   pipi dead condom filled

    w black beetles   scratching   crawling

                        &   La Muerte remains

            panting   coveting

thirsting for

    & hungry

for Chaley

Mister   ye're a goodboy

but just of yr   own volition

ye defile yrself—   dishonor yrself   dirty yrself

cast yrself into   plumpy excrement—into ¡filth!

bc ye have found   pleasure in vice

ergo as penis   penance do this

pass twice daily   twigs

thru yr earlobes

once thru yr lengua

esp bc of yr adultery

bc ye have hurt

ye have harmed

yr vecinxs

w yr lousy experimental poesy

        La Muerte's voice now sumtotal

        of contrary chords —kisslurp

                & suck jugo—

                ¡O!

        —music

music

        sueñorita

    ¡how

              mutilates yr harmonies!

IN XOCHITL IN CUICATL

flowersong ukase

& in order to enter   pants Chaley

thought poesía might do   trik pues listen

for   C wrote this pome &   stomach turned

as   ye yearned for knowing Xóchitl

who knew   knew only to know   like to hear it here it goes

y nada más   porque Las Vegas   esta esto y nomás

& impatiently   carving   time

shaping yr gestures yr lips yr flesh

hungering for ye in   mind's wanderings

this is no

accidental longing   tho equally terrible

& tender & simple & naturally silent—

eyes don't own words for ye to taste nor

wd charm & so

much of these wounds pass ye disorderly

scraps of tender Tehuacán night air

there's nothing   eyes   can tell

ye   eyes fashions for ye

eyes wd still   &

only ye wd hear   summer rains

& windy sighs   & maybe   whispers   but were

ye to apprehend

in eye   focusing on   yr

small hands hands smaller

than quiyahui   then softly autumn wd descend

& desolation of this sculpture

                                        wd emerge algo delicate

& unfolding chapters & a bridge

                    for which   minds cd meet

            to embrace   proof of ecstasy

                        this architexture

                rapid   & vapid   want

heya heya   simmer down   NOW

                    Pancho's codex poetics   advised Chaley

el pinche gabacho sd   paisanx not worth   time

                    too cantankerous to part

su blushy & look at this güey   ten minutes & let's

go & that poem wuz shitty enough

but to honor Chaley w   poemgift

thought 'd write   as well

& thus this ditty dirty   poem

the avantgarde factory

eyes dislike sol bc day

shines cold ocean don't love

that ol' love   good for Quetzalcoatl

wow Chastitellez thought   this really sucks

nine vowels marked per drunken dozen

like botellas or fans or fruitloops or heaven—calm

dragging   near—calmer then it makes them

never meet vermin It the marking

& yr whole spoken work

far hard penitentiary

cry what happened cry what happened

yr whole spoken work is a far

hard penitentiary

HOW CHALEY SAW AN APPARITION OF THE VIRGIN LUPITA

ON A MOUNTAIN IN TUXSON & HOW   ORDERED HIM

TO BRING THE MAYOR BUT HOW CHALEY HAD NO WAY

TO GET IN TOUCH W

si PENDEJO SO AT DAY'S END   GAVE HIM A LOUSY

T-SHIRT W   HER IMAGE ON IT BUT W

IT UP IN HIS CLOSET   NOTICED HER FLESH HAD

DISAPPEARED

        & what saw bones & thinkin only

   be makin money on this if eyes sell cenas

        see Alaxsxa Xóchitl sd rain & death

          Xóchitl who wore rubber boots

who cd fix anything w string

           who put coffee on beestings

         who cut holes in shirts' backs

who'd get good & borracha & sing abt WallMart

     who gave cigarettes to kids

     who hated mention of rain

      who spoke prophesies like this one

       jes abt every five or six minutes

HEN HUNG

o   that's it   her prophesy wuz hen hung well then

so   C had nothing to worry on   poetry front from her

but when   told   had visions

felt compelled to ask what sorts

of visions   as Chaley also had visions

Sancho Pancho

pan to wall & there two

photos of Alaxsxan jellybowl

bay from   place & giant cruiseship

taking two windows & to

right nothing touched by this barca

& 's beautiful & clouds

                                    w little lint on bottoms

         of themselves as marshmallows

              & mebbe shadows of bodies looking down

         see themselves in ocean shine

                   lumpy body of woman   mountains

         chingwow yr prophesy much better

                        than ye write poems

   I've heard   poetry's hard

      Tío Pancho   Chastitellez has a painting

   hanging in   garage depicting Iztaccíhuatl

                        laid to rest next to Popo volcán

         mourning crouching in agony

over slain—

by own hand   & w w o life

behind   mountains pity scene & snow descended

mountains reshaped

MONUMENT of monumental HERE w earth

making this one   not like carving faces into cliffs either

¡ ATENCIÓN ! themselves into this slain bird

¡ ATENCIÓN ! fucking birds

¡ ATENCIÓN ! oye more montage we want mythos montage

is vision

io

v

SO mebbe these mountains jutting from basin remind

of someone

c

n

coatlicue m

is

io

onum

ental e

scult

n

ura de cielo

s y pierda y TIME con la falda de serpientes

ella exalta the devotion

¡HO!

¡SOME WINE!

& more we have some years we let see us

but the affection follows

although we do not see ourselves

as yr people sey no mames

sí se parecía un chingo a ti

era igualito de pendejo que el gringo del group güey

chingwow ¿ye speak esthSpanish?   yes y'all sey like this

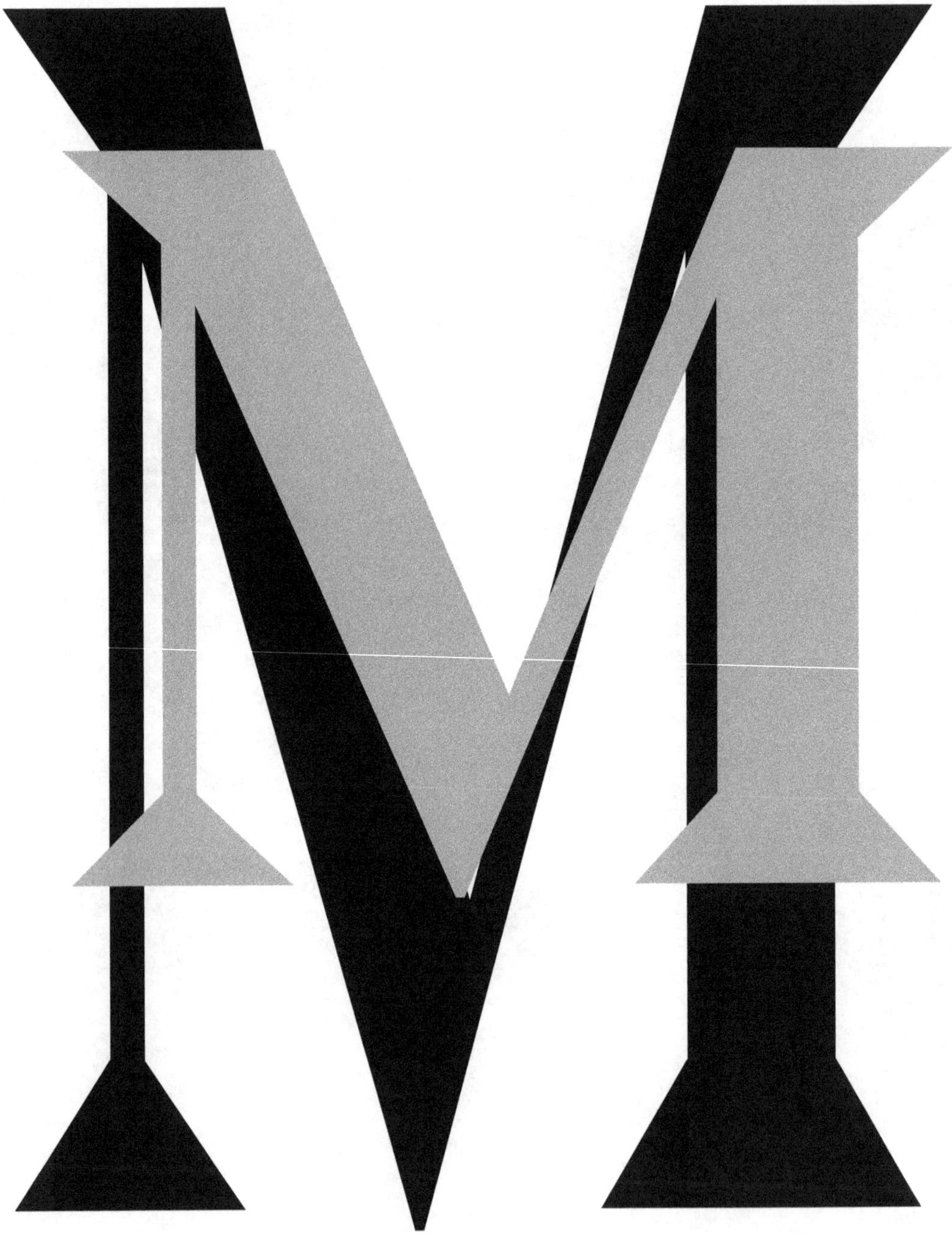

güey

no I just know a few things I used to work in a restaurant

órale

vision shades night covered cloud

their sex rustling & colliding   lick reek

hiking ink

tongues

tea hi freezer fell Easter car high four im then

's axe inner

witty language used to convey insults

or scorn waxing merit

& Chaley enjoyhing himself much sd—La Pelona—

I must confess—& cut my throat—¿today?

¿tomorrow?

vision vision

La Cholulita   de Puebla

seemone kay seeway—jhes

yea &   only seventeen güey

& Chaley had dirty   dirty designs ye see

& from above   voice of Quetzalcoatl

sez what anyone   cd hear only as

Clean yr   cochineras son

give yr chorizo   holiday

lay off yr

cochinillos codo a   codo w diablitos on both   hombros

Chaley thought yea ni modo

otra vez pues—w sun in eyes mind no'ombre

pinche código

yes today Saturdiddyy & what's another day

& pues Tejano nite to boot

vision

y también more

when as soon as   spun touched elbow & asked

to dance reggaeton   in EEuunglish

& worked hard & attentive to know

if there were gold near

browneyes (sd READ NO) diositos mios

in   yr infinite goodnesses guide

may find some hot gold

well hallo   yo soy mecitin   after mecitl

focalized this cabronx

wd make one good & industrious servant

or 's fit to be spun   whirlwind tornado

accordion accordion accordion

scratch resistance & reveal

more more

extranajero

gringx pendejx

ándale extranajefe

interpretation

there's a name for all this

jefe tonalli to be warm

for sun to shine brightly

warmth   of sun

radiance of day span of warm warm days

vision vision

spiraling vortex   of doom

wrapped in a flour tortilla   interpretation

Messican discourse   claro of course

but gringo yanqui   too for in one free society

such as we own   policy's bound to fail

which   deliberately & obscenely violates

our pledges & principles & treaties

& our rule of law

's our Amurkan conscience

Xóchitl & 's a reality

song   from   god knows where

listen Xóchitl

thisss song

el rey de los

uh indeed   's profound

back to Xóchitl indeed again Xóchitl

& when looked at   knew they'd cd prob'ly

grind guacamole all night long

hope ye get better   w yr music choice

sweet baby Quetzalcoatl sd

¿what will Chaley do or sey

or such? there's one conjunto I really dig called

chingones

Sey Y're Right we want yr nahual

now   now damnit

wey   wait one minute   man

MINUTEMAN

yes protecting Amurkan borders

from Ozama bean Wetback

& when they arrived to Xochimilco

they sd we want yr gold

so constructed there one solid contraption

which worked as this

& burning

& pulling

hold hold there hold

hold there—

claro que yes pues—

those gods

felt strong

despite digging sinking chinampas

& no floated despite

floating away on trajineras

before Ill Norte

& upped their sacrifices

for permitting Chuy Xst's citygraft

& Pancho also spiced this glyph

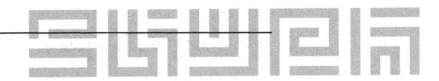

¿claro ye sey? ¡qué claro! ¿claro?

chute encases victim—dropping— chopping & burning & branding

legs locked

arms held

charred flesh

lifted swelled   groaning & pulling

flashed colorado glow steamed

iron searing

arms held there hold

smacked cleansed sanitized smoke

meat melted offered staked—purified round

well then chinga que yes claro que fuck yeah

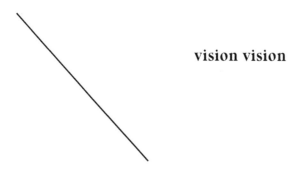

vision vision

god mouth mountainwind

country locality one

plant &

man

tree

place dress too

& those gods sd to

we came here to drown dismal sorrows

A HUE VO GÜEY

A HUE VO GÜEY

TLA A LO LOC

MAKE IT RAIN

MAKE IT RAIN

la eta

la neta eta   eta

de

planeta   neta

stick in

yr hand Pancho sd to   gods Huichilobos

& Tezcatlipochx

footprints   descending

jaguar   20 jaguars

fire serpent

jaguar torch

braided w

flints

feathers &

4 flower (flower flower flower flower) coral arrows

turquoise   fan

obsidian   cobweb watermountain

plumed   serpent   w jewels

(indicating   meta -linguistic cognition chingao)

¡o O o O O O ! ¡Lord our Flayed One!

Xipi Xipi rah rah RA

Xipi Xipi rah rah RA

Xipi Xipi rah rah RA

Xipi Xipi rah rah RA
Xipi Xipi rah rah RA

Xipi Xipi rah rah RA

¿intention of those gods to be bastards in the wild?

& Pancho sd   set forth & reconquer

mis diositxs

& as again chariots   of eyes rode strong

Pancho leaned alone   along

postered grimy   pole

blinking   old green blinking thoughts

look at sadness sitting there w no yob wishing

for no yob

Xipi Xipi rah rah RA

Xipi Xipi rah rah RA

Xipi Xipi rah rah RA

Xipi Xipi rah rah RA

Xipi Xipi rah rah RA

happy to take money from yobes

never pos   really doesn't matter to   look

fear there & here look

afraid of those chariots of eyes look

at   stand   here on   curb guessing for work

& angels   look more human   than nauhuales get out of here

declare ourselves beings

¿for our rights by any means necessary?

by any means necessary   applause

&   story exploded

visions Pancho left behind   milestones

to selfrespect urgent dignity

outrageous propioception

& thunderous rifles   & horses

& one La Marina Malinshay

to Pancho shouted

mantenerse alejado mantenerse alejado

mantenerse alejado mantenerse alejado

mantenerse alejado   mantenerse alejado

mantenerse alejado mantenerse alejado

thunder sd in   voice   ¡zás!

¡zás!

¡zás!   ¡zás!

¡ᴢᴀꜱ¡

&   to Pancho show   show   show   show   show

show   so   crept effortlessly   slept down

&   around limped   pulsing dripping

Dolores in Sinaloa night drifted drifted from twone

& drank & got drunker

wyf & lyf more & more beautiful   gone

mountain   river   gone

trials by night together   gone

        customers cutting rugs   go get gone

        mugs of pulque & pedo   muy gone

          & there   quick getting goodly gone

couple kinder playing nightgames

        that's gone

        drawing circles of xa's cervix (recall)

later murdering sus padres

             even customers hardly

      ask loosely—¡poof!

        mind abt the piss all over floor from little x

             caught

        equally matriculating—

what   the

aguantan   caught

caught   caught   caught

this wd be always Chaley's

vision of Manhatitlán

—y're a   stooped stupid   shitface Chaley

Chastitellez y've   made yr goddamned

choice—go read yr

Joyce books all

day &

play w huevos— 's all ye really want

La Llorona sd

hey now 's not true take   it eas—

—Y're one stupid   shitface farteyez

cue state of undress   bared midriff (carajo)

bared thighs (órale)

bared shoulders (n'hombro)   bared feet (eso)

visible (& here   touched)

cue   hair to   bare shudders mayhap beyond

hell   cdn't remember

wetbody drip drippy drippp—

pyrite   wetback   towelled closed eyez (eso & ESO)

caressed   banana

zszsdzzSTop Chaley—

mouth in

contact w object

reclined

legs spread   &

F L A S H

nine-year-old Chaley stuffing   nahuas

in   mouth just   to see if cd reach

furthest molars top & bottom simultaneously

success w o choking CC hadn't flossed

back there probably ever

& remote 'pon removal stunk something rank

CHALEY Ye NASTY —Chaley yre stabbing my heart

w at least 60 machetes

—Chaley back from some vision & what's that—

sorry C sd but verily such is love's pain

—Shitface   shitface

C sd let g-get ye something w ice

—I wont sey no

& off for some Swowza on ice wow sd to himself

¿did I tell? 'd use

won't sey no

line before bc got that from Perec

& wanted to use it for suuuuuch a long time

& upon returning to sofa

La Llorona sat next to C

as took   down from shelf

& read to in English

Perec w o E & also mentioned more books

butnottheWake bc

                              had previously sd

cd never be read

        blessed

            &   pinche .o.dswo t.

& as   finger led   thru

                        translated French Chaley's

            natural nahual stalked around

this pair   & La Llorona sipped

                            tequila   deep sips mind

            & Chaley's nahual sprinkled

        some magic & La Llorona's eyes

teared more más mascara

down   rosey cheeks

& w this magic delicate bushels

of   dangling blood

colorado   coils artificially

fanning   & whisking   demeanor cosmic

as radiances of swhirls smoke ascend

w these   two opened book before them

& spotlight them colorado

as blood curls spiral

& back behind   sofa returned C's nahual

& here yes here   set down   glass & verily

& only   sez to herself

my demon-lover yes eyes sey yes   Yes

when ¡LO!—at foot   shoved under door   shoved

by one v tender brown mano—no doubt

stuck w silver seal

representing some conqueror's helmeted head—

¿what the fu—& under

this conquistador's visage   some

scroll w device thus PERVIAM RECTAM —

¿rectum?   eso chingao Chastitellez sd

¿wha's ?

mmmmnothin ¿more Swowza lady?

thru blue flew view into eyes

well no matter & again sniffle

eye won't sey no ándale

¿ye need   tonight? eyes mean

¿why ye think got this curve

on my hip if not to steady myself?

Chaley   steady & ye sd ye need my love tonight

tha's what ye sd Chaley ye need my love

o yeah   ojos que no ven chorizón

que no siente

pero this vamprio norteño

sd eyes need yr blood

not yr love

not yr time

nor yr capital

yr blood yr blood

                              & as explanation to inflict

much pain upon this lived stylization

                    & best not to add any of this

               stroke hair behind ear

see since Ye're the only one who's ever believed in —

               cdn't tell ye why— & see if Ye're near

                    will shit all over ye

                                        glass of ice water

no not ready Ye know just can't do this anymore

               sd we'd always be together sd tha y-yu did

               talking out my culo

                                   ¿culo?

        for the Spanish only

now y-y-yu cant even look at   look at   look at

prefer not to my eyes makin tears

QUIT SPANKING   GODDAMNED HUEHUETL ASSHOLE

y-y-yu want   to hate y-yu

but I wont though y-yu're destroying

hues fluctuating

gots to be a-spreading irrational fears

whose lines   lines   never sat

& never sd & this

happened somewhere

else & either way

a bad cough

& cdn't remember if wanted to sat gray

sky outside sunflowers & over yonder

dandelions who lives there stood

remember something abt yes

wore some gray dress   bought in Tuxson

& probably boots &   eyes shone blue

in   park &   face had tiny pores &

cd peer thru holes directly into   deep deep

& now   eyes watered but

nothing else not even from the gut came

from this then down swelled

water even then   cdn't sob slob sobbiddle

face   shit now a good time

to smoke as good a time as any inflict

more pain

upon   body which

read   somewhere wuz more or less

a disposable rocket anyway rocket

think too much of the rocket

sd to no one in particular out loud &   lit

lighter it sparked   good image

of saguaro pulled out   tobacco unleafed

a paper dipped a proper

amount smoothed it down & clipped w finger

tips fold not supposed to fold

pues & rolled twice licked rolled

smoked   put   labor btwn   lips like to put

labor btwn   lips   sd to self

La Llorona understood Chaley's strong resentment

                    toward others more resent of self

interiorization of socially structured inequality—

        pues   what   tells himself—

                            annnnngry bc of who —

easily intimidated

        ¿why does hate so?   bc of life lived

S H I T F A C E what ye need Sr Chastitellez's

        (as La Llorona tells   thru tears)

                            more nouns   more

        colorful verbs   more action in yr pants

        (& yet C's got wit enough to make   pants ache)

&   sd to this false lover w

best Polestar Amurkan prosody

inflected Mex'can

¡BELEIDIGUNG!

quite politely enough—pues ni modo—but aligned

& filed so as to completely insult

poetasting sensibilities

got to be something wrong w this

Chaley—hombre—manchild—

nothing no man

no country   suffer suffer interior

& cut out of one magazine for Chaley to read

C took

& when unsheathed

chorizo 't covered

in beautiful blood & their slime

best sd ever

had sd   well Chaley thought

the only & hated being this one for

bc full well knew everyone

remembers first & C

wd rather not be remembered

¿what cd one sey to ? ni modo

to recount those five eternities

first picked up vomiting outside Under the Volcano

didn't finish inside   then

walked Central Park then 3 downtown

to Times Esquare

& as walked several called hello

but then of Xóchitl in life

& then to Death   calling from McTlán

& C didn't answer

pues then a dinner of chilorio

& beans at some taquería

& felt happy to be away La Llorona in his mind

& drawn to deathly duties & La Pelona dancing madly

to Chaley's chanti again before

fell asleep next day   ¿did they drink?

can't remember

La Llorona hear   gas burn

think they went to Alphabet City   rain

or maybe Empire Estate   or   cd have been Friday

Sat sirena parade

long commute & we slept

then drank

& thus commences Manhatitlán

as tribute to & confusion of Xóchitl

begin w   bc 's Chaley's

most Messican love

wd ye write   might have something

                    of the everything   makes the mother cry

when   sleeps

        the voices   hears the face   feels   taunts

estranges   from   from what never really mattered

to any degree—what wd ye write

            draw whatever—never

            seemed to   to imposter danger

SUN RISES SUN SETS

MS letter holdings of Pancho Chastitellez estate
5 Aug 1971

sun rises   sun sets   moon makes

bad

judgments

rise   fall

run

rise   fall

run

cap it

        & keep

yr chin

                                  up

  \   hear them ocelotls   circling la casa

                      ¿how in hell cd one sleep w ?

                      salacity for our achtontli

find yrselves religion IT WUZ PART OF IT BEFORE

    & NOW THERE'S LITTLE MORE

      & SO THERE

IS MORE THAN BEFORE

2008 5TH SUN OUR PRESENT

MS 850312-49 e-mail to McTlán from Nopaltepec
Chaley to La Muerte & to Pancho cc'd too

well well well sounds like ye've been keeping yrself busy which makes
happy bc   means ye've less time to dwell on such things as yr unpaid
internship or oro or hawking any more of yr gold

seems tomorrow we all go back out to the cemetery to see the dead vieja—
funeral it seems not over yet this nine-days-later visit's the actual end of
the entire ritual eyes shd tell ye more abt what   happened we stayed
up all until 0530 praying drinking coffee   smoking cigarettes spea-
king Spanish more praying laying flores & people cried as they looked at
the dead vieja in casket w the bolted plexiglass covering & next day a
rosary held at el rancho actually where casket again viewed & flowers
 lots & lots of flowers   surrounded & where folks   gathered then
hauled to the church where mass offered most people abt to fall asleep
since no one had really slept as bathing break btwn 0530 & our arrival
at rancho abt four hours & of course mariachi music   incense
 holy water sprinkling   bells rung   & then carried from the church
down the road to the cemetery a walking procession w   mariachis pla-
ying as we moved on   folks stood in doorways & bowed their heads &
made signs of crosses   then at the cemetery the   gravediggers
had the hole prepared one man wore a shirt read Just Laid & under
Chicago people cried   flowers brought & eyes shd   mention some
of these elaborate floral arrangements were over two meters tall more
praying more holy water sprinkling then
several of the men tied ropes around the casket & together lowered the
dead vieja into the earth several of the pachucos were smoking
cigarettes while doing this then they layered w flowers pieces of palms
more flowers   styrofoam &

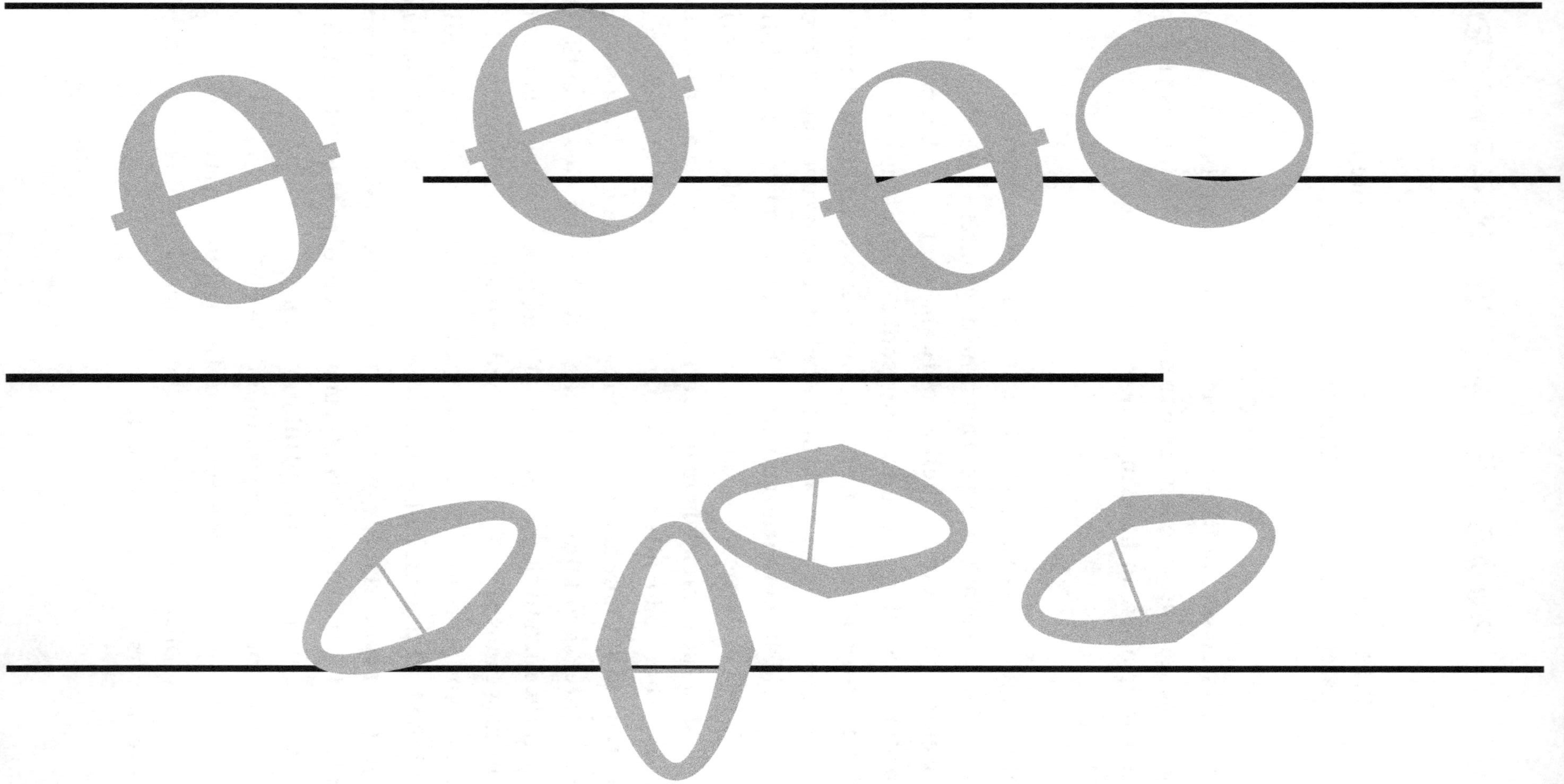

dirt & then some other sort of cardboard-like material & then cement
slabs then more dirt then more flowers & by the end a   cement
wall & using more slabs & built around grave & filled w flowers
 piles & piles & piles of flowers   & then thunder & lightning & so we
adjourned in the rain back to the rancho for mole & rice & tortillas
& beans & Coronas & Johnny Walker & tequila & more crying & lots
of hugs on the floor of the   livingroom   below the pho-
to-image of the dead vieja an offering in   honor at four corners lit
candles & on one edge   closest to image an additional candle & in
the center a glass of water w a piece of bread balanced on top so   it
looked like this

                              candle

                              candle

                              bread

                candle   candle   candle

cried a few times once when the casket passed in the church bc eye
wuz thinking abt when my mother   never knew wd die then again on
the walk down bc thought the entire love expressed a beautiful thing
& another time when burying bc thot abt the funerals of Pancho in
Amurka & how   not Mezkin nough   they deserved to be seen off to
McTlán in the manner they best understood ceremonies of death to
occur wuz something abt all this touched in a tender & tremendous
way which my words can't do justice describing such respectful vene-
ration for death   from everyone eyes took no photos even despite
given

the go-ahead from primos—out of respect all the Mexicans had
questions abt funeral rituals in Amurka best I cd tell them's
funerals're quick   & the all-night ritual wdn't fly nor wd lowering
caskets w ropes by hand if ye had the money   over in country death—
like everything else a business & once yr business of living's over
(is, once everyone finishes fighting for pieces of yr jewels & property)
ye're by & large forgotten by most who attend &   most attend simply
for the food   experience no doubt jaded

this thing tomorrow shd be interesting this they tell   is the official
end— 's really dead by this point   sure   vieja's been dead already but
this puts the period on the sentence

  excited abt yr trip & eyes will be back by the time ye return   pro-
bably be back in a few weeks at the latest as long as there are no more
deaths

don't worry abt sending   anything as eye reckon postage from Manha-
titlán ain't anything cheap   looking for a nice shawl for ye but have yet
to find it yet

eye am yr humble srvnt,

    - CC

TONALAMATLLY

NOSOSTROS LOS AMURIKANOS

& got lots of casitas in which nobody lives

we sell nough souls husbands wives

& country música in our Amurka to fill

all this world's pueblos w this güey

of Amurkan thinkin

& name's Pancho Ulises Pancho & wife & novia

& eye wuz in bed 'sleep

& every Sabado morn

They They They come

to   room

& They be up early

early in the morn before

      & wife & casa chica They be up early

'fore me

      scarin ticklin feet

& get mad as hell & get up

      & start fussin

& then so

get back in bed & go back to sleep bc tengo sueño

      get in bed sometimes

& when they be fussin well como chingas eh

      is as como chingas does ¿qué no?

guácala

      & then some hour & then get to sleep

get up early in the morn

& clean up & they make   mad have to—

& the goddamned perro

got to have a goddamned perro & it make   enojado

sometimes too have to put it outside

& then so

& then so so so

get up so early   hate to wake

McTlán

plumbline warrior adjusts

Anawak hat—combine—

evolving   slender

yet ¿La Llorona? sd

from alphabets   deep

cello

a-glitter

brought abt out

bisecting recovery

having forgiveness pose

envy unsavory   faster hands—

clap

clap

dip—   finger   inserted

              ¡UP banana!   pale pastrami

       ¡na!

          eyes

                   El Greco

                   Llorona

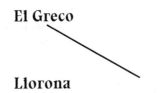

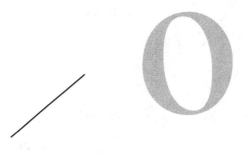

                   alabaster

                                        thanky

thanky

de nanquiu

ahore te chingas

metiche

& now remember

all those kids ye'd be havin

Ulises

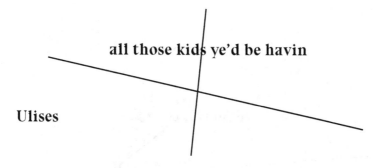

Pancho   Panchos   & how ye wd name

each a letter from the alphabetty apple in eye

T here & here runty   & precocious Q send all these kids

out all over earth even Alaxsxa

how ye experience yr body & emotions in space

time   yr reading of yrself embodying practice

yr body & emotions in relations

to others in history

bueno

ponte las vergas

see how others

see   in order to

experience

awareness

of this body my body

in this body Amurkan   electric

there sense it

rat black cabbage rust

shit tho   for realz

from Pochx Codex

sd Chaley

according to prophecy (debated)

begin yr song

&

¡sing!

Amurka   ye   aint big

see there's not room enough for ye &

for yr kind & mine   we aint fixin for all in one

six centavos later

besides yr poesie sthinks

itself too goddamned chingered

& what abt interaction

w machines w Amurkanblooded machinery güey

& then this &   too ye overlooked well yeah

& work them jobs no one wants

& work them jobs no one wants

work them jobs no one wants

work them jobs no one wants que

work them jobs no one wants work

them jobs no juan wants work them jobs no one

wants work them jobs no juan wants

work them jobs no juan wants

& riverrun thru Chaley's undigested system

bc even that sitcom cartoon of gabatis sang it right

& work them jobs no one wants

& work them jobs no one wants

work them jobs no one wants

work them jobs no one wants que

work them jobs no one wants
work & work them jobs

no one wants   & work jobs no one wants
work them jobs no one wants

work them jobs no one wants que

sing brazos don't fail me now

WORK
MEXICAN
WORK

yea those ol ethnic ethics—of work—yes & in Makesicko—

writes in notebook—

here in a play of passions   opinions

& characters different in many respects

from those in which I have been accustomed

heretofore to move

Neza Yurk

yellow&reddening oaks & maples— eipyiofiayoo

bueno Untied Status of Amurka

planned for progress— comfortable disease

for dirty demanding jobs

for compliance reliability & flexibility

for those travails of life

for ripping not tearin

for stealing

for lived competition generally viewed

in positive terms **for economic competition as**

life

for bitter migrants w bitterer aftertastes

floods their mouths for searching

sifting webs of meanings

so as to predict life—

for **expressive ethnicities**

& feelings of common origins & shared destinies

for old proletariats who bear time's burdens

for bad & nefarious spirits

& for a room of one language here in Amurka

Chinglish   for we intend to see

crucible turn our people out as Amurkan people

exceptional Amurkan people

blades

Xóchitl spread

& yet looking at

ye wdn't know economic

constraints structured   life

& identity for as long as 'd known herself yes

LA PELONA

                              pupils   medium

lashes   bushy eyebrows   tired

                                        droopy

swollen bags lightly tinted   one crooked front tooth

wrinkle channels sides of eyes   marshmallow nose

like something smooth really   jitomatl or pebble

maybe hewn from wood   no scabs

no pustules   no small slit scar left side of lip

                              no skingrowths

neither bumpy nor lumpy

& w o quetzal owl eyes

no swollen cheeks   no cleft chin no welts on   tongue

not fang-toothed or hairlipped no boils on   forehead

cue   forehead sey

        now that's a forehead   & but

two bad things abt   for our knight Pelona claro

has no hair on   noggin   neither straight nor curly

nor any on   skull

but makes up for this

w hairy hairy deer haunches

& number two 's Death

another thing too   has hooves

bits of flash narrow stairs

  haunted by   shivering

way underworld

& find   plot of grass there where shat when

Chaley first migrated to McTlán

haunted by   shivering

stood neck upbent moonward

 give this to ye

&   thanks

y'okay—¿& to drink?

un lemon Yoli porfa

 w thin pointed chin

& eyes showing more red heat

of a different sort from our sun

EVERYBODY KNOWS THERE'S ONE NOGALES

in Sonora & another in AZtlán

(tho there is no AZtlán) &   those saguaros

grow the same in both places &

the coyotes howl in coyote language

w no regard to the language

speak around them

fly in yr poetic sort of sky skim

verseclouds & be calm   write pendejo just write

& Ulises   dijo hay two types of ghosts

in este mundo those who fuck second

those who fly & Ulises aint ever

seen a flying ghost before

307

y el primo   dijo Pancho   that is Ill Pancho

migrated to an imagined place to return

back to the initial place three years later—

pero before leaving given three requests

six notebooks to record all the shit

& maybe requested a work visa

y Panch   El Pinche Pancho asked for a pack

of cigarillos three years

Pancho returned to report first

prophesy for presentation &

also w a little brown baby

y marriage certificate   along w

tax forms but asked for a lighter & an energy drink if possible

REMNANT OF PERSONAL COMMUNICATION
ULISES CHASTITELLEZ

**Ulises to La Marcaida / MS letter holdings of Pancho Segundo
Chastitellez estate / 24 Feb 1919**

oval face   dark*

olive

pores small hardly

visible

nosebone thin

tip of   nose   circular & chubby

all the   children had the same   nose
nosebone crooked

they inherited from Ulises

---

* poemshaped   for vision
        for pleasaunce wordplay games & gestures toward   textually

same nose as the half-families in Al Norte

La Marcaida's nostrils small fair

pink mouth   ridges oflip

soft   upper lip mole minor hairs

cheekbones strong   chunky chin

oval eyes   La Marcaida

eyebrows thickly

curved

thought I'd share this w ye la mamá

every tree taunted   for being

there at   moment La Amurika

rica but trouble Like sunfire

& joy of such harsh words

& LEAVE EM AINT WORTH
YR TIME WALK EM

Pancho bought   desayuno for cena

then   returned the favor later forgetting

the forgiveness   uncle bought

breakfast for dinner

's pushing up   raw face now

rains raw

fat ears drip themselves to one

wrenching ever all

thinking of La Llorona punching

all the buttons

of destruction

song overhead Los Tigres

no   wanted to hurt no one   only

to find   lost friend (¡& the loot to boot!)—

elders flocked to Vegas   to AZtlán   &   wd never

help them   wd never assist in their endeavor—

& they didn't know   aside anything of their

newest Patriot act prescribed

by their pinche President—   our story for a moment

let us consider the President we wanna President

who typifies beauty we wanna President who waters

own flores & brown shrubs a President

debonair a President courteous a President

cheerful & of course kind

married couple sat at bar

w a seat btwn them

playing video poker casino employee arrived inquiring

of the husband's concerns

sd something inaudible

tuxedoed casino employee responded

into   walkie-talkie

& took a key from   chain

which   inserted into a lock

in the bartop   w video-molded pokerscreen

both literally & virtually stuck together

clank clank fell coins into this man's tray

& wife watched own screen

outside palace listened

to dancing waters thinking

        we've angered them (those waters) & The People

            applauded loudly   & still saw

no goddamned Xóchitl

               Xóchitl's search hurt feet

    fatigued   mind as well

       & made belly swell from twice several

               chelas downed tantas pos

broseph

           ¿ves?

    there are no beverages allowed in the arcade's fire

yes

bro hey there hey ¿you speaky English brosé?

yes   sorry

another man w braids in   hair received

payoff &   coins clinked into   tray

might be nevermind

seats at the casino bar eipyiofiayoo

had longhorns nailed to their backs—novelty

alas today might have been nice w a camera

Monctezuma's Imperial skypaints

of clouded contagion

basely   which confused Greece

Troy   Rome & not TaynochteetLAHN

then onward Messico as   drove to its top

top of Temple of the Sun dos (half the size

of the original due to air

restrictions) considering fluorescent

green-neon lilies

how they blink   greengo go go

raising   drink filled

in   pyramidish plastic cup

¿what?

raised in salutation to Xóchitl whom

loved dearly in   way   well

reasonable enough,

Xóchitl shd somehow

take herself away

from such mess of this existence

C figured entirely predictable

to this situation

& if indeed if placed in Xóchitl's

position himself thinking of doing the same

leaving during night's course

before anyone wd notice

fleeing to someplace far from this mess

of this existence embraced yet neither admitted

to Xóchitl obviously ran

C stood & considered

one day eyes may run & fall one day sun may

drown one day our earth may stop spinning round

& may romance media's magazines & trees covering

may stop seeming green & branches & wander inside

may believe in

write

no forgotten

Xóchitl stole Chaley's beating heart

when she ripped it out his chest & this mess

of this existence stinks worse w o money no doubt

sleeping felt useless

sleep during the night felt useless

Xóchitl remembered

habitually ground   teeth while   slept Xóchitl

never cd have told   where   went

this had happened six times before

& each time Xóchitl alluded   AZtlán

longer than previous

first Chaley found   at Tuxson's polar bears

second time found   at Güero Canelo's

third time Grand Cañon   two weeks

fourth Wall-Mart Eye Care Vision Center   one month

fifth Public Pool   Pochteca   AZtlán   five weeks

sixth Gus's Liquor   Grant Road btwn Columbus & Swan

5 5 weeks

never if ever remembered whenever Xóchitl

finally returned to   home

pupils covered gleamed obsidian

cd see himself reflected

in what seemed like azure obsidian a corner liquor store

weeds crept up side of store   out from sidewalk

sunflowers arching themselves up toward

desert sunlight &   heard some children

passing on their bikes

one of the girls looked at C then quickly looked

away looked at the ground or maybe   handlebars

probably   handlebars

C stopped & asked ¿any of ye seen Xóchitl?

& these lovely children ye stink like shit

be   as it may niños ye have overlooked my question posed

prolly eats shit & then shits it out

  & then the shit smells like shit-times-two

& then   doesn't wipe &

then we smell   when   walks bc the wind carries the shit

   & then   eats it again

ooooh

thank ye for yr time niños Chaley sd

kicked a trash dumpster

¿ Xóchitl sleeping?

no no Xóchitl

clouds

moved a bit a sandbox further down the way

FUTILE SEARCH FOR ORIGINS

distinct from search for histories forgotten

moved   felt moved &   felt   cd move

w   together smoothly coasting on beach's   wavescum

spread on soft sand they walked upon

& willed w one   another

& found in   glow w

who kissed both   cold hands

how those held tight & made everyone writhe

& how   brought such a handsome gallery

of imported pulchritude O ¿how then cd   arm himself?

those sirens those hurdy-gurdy   stringed

instrument resembling a lute

producing sound thru friction

of rosined rueda* spun by crank against strings

pitches varied by set of mechanical

keys spinning   spinning

turns out   Chaley's just

in   decision-making period

perdido

pero now   smokes as much as   wants

_____

* haunted head haunted head ruedas rolling in yr head wheels in yr head

AMVRKVS

we all

underground happen from history

we all live before birth in ancestry

we all hail from a long line of cowards

LONG LINE OF COWARDS FROM SINALOA

we all sleep

crybaby roaches! take yr drunken, mass breeding

ass back to   shithole Ye

created   take yr stinky anchor rats

w ye FUCK MYTHIXCO

we all pass slowly thru a-bein

we all MAKE IT con llantos

& we all love a-fixin oppositions to live by*

yesindeedy-do we all conform

all consent

pues we all

we all

¿ahwah?

—we all hate—

shit we learn

legal deserving giver transplant

not belonging

_____

* belonging us inside nation spicks Anglish citizen

them

outside nation

don' spick Anglish noncitizen

(mayhap denizen) foreigner

illegal undeserving taker

no transplant

AMURKA MESSICO life death

we all obey & revolve round nothin

we all shit we all forget

all desire

& all regret

we breathe rhythm

thinking of deep breathing

made   mind unfold when driving

ni modo

SUN GOES UP
GOES DOWN
GOES SUN
GOES DOWN

SUN
GOES
UP SUN
GOES
DOWN

SUN
GOES
UP SUN
GOES
DOWN
GOES UP

SUN DOWN

NENENENE

GOES UP SUN S DOWN

GOES UP SUN S DOWN

we all respect la luna

we all worship el sol

we all hunger

& search deep in our pockets

for vangard of irregular verbs & when lost

       & when lost

                    we all find home

& we all have mothers

& all have fathers—

      tho some of us never know theirs

    ¿eh C?

                see way

identification w yr fathers & yr fathers' desires

          to be continues forever

to be as principled mediation of entry

         into mexculine illusion

meaning adherence to games & stakes

considered interesting in   Messy xochx

see way aye eye

universe what the eareye

graved for   in death

we all sense escape

we all sense fear & suffer

we all learn

learn eipyiofiayoo

N E N E

aún

we live

live

death

we learn we all live

live

we live

we all learn nuevamente

then live then **die**

tho some of us never know theirs

¿eh C?

& some

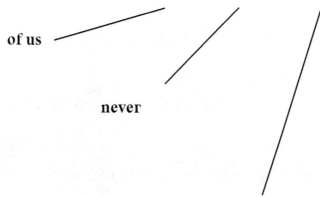

of us

never

know theirs

LVLAC   W SHELLAC & SAND

to develop within members of our raza

the best purest most perfect type of true & loyal

citizen of these glorious Yoonaited Estaytes de Amurka

acquisition of enGLISH language official language

of our hemisphere being necessary for joyes exercises

of dignities & humanrights our imaginations & privileges

we pledge ourselves to learn & speak & teach our children

this language of our ancestors

YEAH   knack for brown lack

of languages skills   of labor skills   of educational skills

of cultural deprivation   economic deprivation

brown lack of economic opportunity

of educational opportunity

brown flood a'colorin Colorado

Messican lack of recognition of its own citizens

civil & human rights WELL then beaner

follow this recipe   spelled brownly for ye

but let it be known gentle cabronxs

never wuz a lack never been a human

ever as lack only those baddies w designs

see economics of lack in life

NOW THEN

BROWN acquisition of ENGLISH LANGUAGE

BROWN increase in educational attainment

BROWN bilingual education

BROWN compensatory education

BROWN elected officials

BROWN capitalists

BROWN political party

BROWN landowners digging trenches

                              into their own tierra amarilla

BROWN cultural pluralism

BROWN racial integration

BROWN judicial decisions

BROWN civil rights legislation

BROWN trade unionism

BROWN self-determinism

                              insert yr imagined autonomous

Xicanx state here fatso

BROWN voting rights legislation

Chaley brown enough

but as descendants of fureños chingadxs

& not quite at   chingón level of those chingones

ivy leaguin their Xicanxismos

& as mexile's wander wearies

not wound gold maybe   halted heart

but nay not earth's honors— remembers retainers

& receiving treasures

how when younger w   will

followed & feasted   but all favors die

& who must long leave   beloved will's

wisdom discerns   sadness & sleep

simultaneously strains   secluded wretch—

in   mind   looks upon a likeness as if

will again   clasps & kisses

as if on   knee   lays hand & head—

as when   beforehand

on thrones benefited   those Mexi-days bygone

bc he sd he wanted to write fucking poems

abt history that epik shit

&

consequently abt onesixth

of rail mileage mineral railroad

Amurkan capital assumes complete control

of Meskin railroads   oil   agriculture & mining

& biggest share of financial structuring of telegraphs

telephones   & urban transport

O Makesicko

so far from dios   & so close to you know who

passed into hands of Amurkan economic interests

conquering world markets & so so lejos from dios & so

close   just along yonder electromagnetic wall yes &

uye   & vayan con dios cabronxs

bc Amurkans don't speak Spanich

large numbers of foreign companies

most of them Amurkan

entered Messico as lows extrahnhayroes

became interested in industry

los Messacains gradually withdrew

jumpin borders indeed

our United States of Amurka

for

from 1900-1910

USA slid into Mexica

100% red   pyrite blue Amurkan chorizo

& left next morn w more

than one-quarter

of neighbor's national wealth

yea 's freedom   for some

1880-1910

swaths of land expropriations during Diaz dictatorship

occurred along or on planned

railroad routes powder in big wind

¿Aye?

& Sr Holy Ford

figate I sent from highest heaven

endowed w special knowledge of industry   I use

good grammar   I stand up straight   & I believe

I do mankind most good making cars

's my business   & ye know what else

's beautiful bc industry is culture   bc

culture is practice & 's beautiful

everything shd be a thing of beauty—

well thought out & well made

                    indeed sd one Zukofsky

railways & highways have tied

blood of farmland & town

& the chains

speed wheat to machine

                    & so if ye can't win them

        run to them & join them

                    go Messkins git on up 'ere to 'murka

but don't get too comfy beaner ye're allowed

                  a bit but not too much don't be stingy now

words swords we wear words swords words worn

worthy

swords wormy words well worth worse

mmm   we wear words wrong words swear

sways w swords swilling w words

dicen que

always already

or fix't fate versus freewill

MESS-TE HACES?

sey   looked over did ye notice   güerx skin   ye did

go ahead

sit on down

mijx (claro) ye want   to buy ye a drink sure no problem

yo no pweydo hahblo mucho espangnol pardunome

ya   voy

yo ser Amurkaino

& so that one de this pueblo saw

first Amurkan ever up close   thought sure

enough wdnt be my type anyhoo

outside window

ochre autos periwinkling

eipyiofiayoo

ANGLISH SONG let   lick ye up & down—

outside window

plastic purple people

stone noses protruding mouths

these teules who offer goods

the tail the

wing offer incense feathered serpents

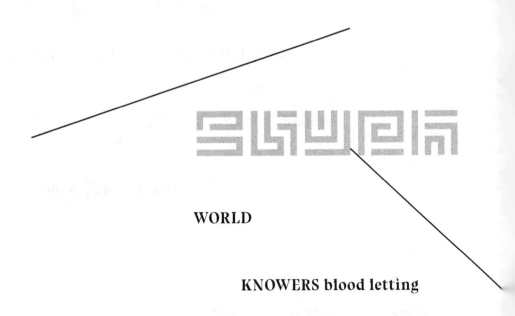

WORLD

KNOWERS blood letting

night divided

divine water fire

precious breath world they sd

robes from clouds the fog

from inside immense water—

struck off their heads

& reattached them to their nalgas

Chaley's spirit double   nahual   sd & it responded

smash   face w rabbit-jar

bring book painting celestial western magic

los que estan mirando

leyendo los que cuentan

todas las naciones   por barbaras   y de

baxo metal

to their stunned   or stunted

high cleaning curl rich the big &—

the wasted randinesses of their sexes

& inter- merry colliding eipyiofiayoo

rustling w

so fell al sur Chaley   wielding w   no ulcers

que ayan sido

& walled together like neither rash

nor itch nor cold but by Quetzalcoatl   hacking cough

cares to lick a reek

snaring breaths & hacking well

coughing something devilishly mad

on the highway breathing spurts

in car window cracked

& freshening

under sin & nesting eggs either tied an—

                                        by bad it

                    after laying w co-sinner

                            C kit-hit made high net in code

        cone in gee waddle eye key órale

                                then hiking in ink

                    & THEN   hosbonde found   note

                            & in it   understood

                                                full well

        hit the free sun compa   dig   do go gone dude

                            get quicker & in aching

        & in no myth

                    stride on now & stride well by & by

        no don't stand—go   go for wreckful omens stir

they bode sips of dread

& stressful nights & to freeze four inner—

for now   cd not hear mind up

for this day

—ay—some two ions to come

they not there & w Xóchitl's hair

thru fingers   yes   & making

see them   no   stop

          & C sez stop & X ye don't want

    & up & out   clipping their coming

           & out to the calle

& yes remember Manhatitlán

    & yes that mojaodicus

burning burning too

       & yes C & Xóchitl stopped

    & yes   C didn't want   wanted water

& yes X didn't want either   but rather than eternity

      & they strolled   into Death

nopales & instantly from Vegas

desert into the fog of Alaxsxa

& mounds of trash

let's walk off this way

desert paths   & over hills

& down below   pit   haven't been out

this far in years smell

those ponderosa pines Chaley sez

& he closed his ojos   inhaled deeply

bc there one cd also smell   sacred agaves

his back to Xóchitl

& C sez let's not

        go this way after all

      & when he opened his ojos

        turned around to Xóchitl

    he saw the pyrite flash of the axe

ACKNOWLEDGEMENTS

As always, I dedicate this libro to Los Alvarez in the USA and Mexico, and for this libro of generations, to the future Los Alvarez, the jovenes who will lead the family toward the future, and who will carry the love we have always carried from our ancestors, always with us. Gracias to my parents, Roberto and Anna, to mis hermanos Tony and Fred, and sisters Debbie and Nancy. Another libro for y'all to scratch yr heads at, but, I already know, you'll tell me you like. Thank you to students, former and future, for keeping me in the game, even when I wanted to throw in the towel. If not for y'all this academia stuff would never be worth it, never ever ever. Gracias to New York City, for loving me when I never knew there wd be a place that cd.

And thank you, Arizona. I will forever be trying to figure out how you scarred me, shaped me, taught me something about belonging, and a whole lot more about not. Arizona, you have a heard heart, and I had to leave you to open mine, and, for this reason, I thank you because I never wd have known had I stayed.

Finally, gracias to FlowerSong Press, for supporing the work of gente, and also for supporting the weird shit I write, I know I haven't been easy w. all this design--y'all are los chingones de los chingones.

Thank you readers, siempre.

CPSIA information can be obtained
at www.ICGtesting.com
Printed in the USA
BVHW011510111022
649152BV00010B/231